A Register of

Territorial Force Cadet Units

1910 – 1922

by

R. A. WESTLAKE

A Register of

Territorial Force Cadet Units

1910 – 1922

by

R. A. WESTLAKE

The Naval & Military Press Ltd

Published by

The Naval & Military Press Ltd
Unit 5 Riverside, Brambleside
Bellbrook Industrial Estate
Uckfield, East Sussex
TN22 1QQ England

Tel: +44 (0)1825 749494

www.naval-military-press.com
www.nmarchive.com

INTRODUCTION

Cadet units were first sanctioned by the Government in 1863 when in that year *Volunteer Regulations* directed that groups of cadets could be formed in connection with existing volunteer companies and battalions.

The "Army Cadet" had, however, existed unofficially for many years, one of the earliest records being of a company of boys on the Isle of Wight, "skirmishing" before King James 1.

In 1908 and the introduction of the Territorial Force those cadet corps formed within Public Schools were invited to join the newly created, Officers Training Corps. The OTC, which later became the Combined Cadet Force, had been formed under the direct control of the War Office for the purpose of supplying officers, both to the Regular and Auxillery forces.

It was not until 1910 that the remaining school and open cadet units of the Volunteer Force were catered for by the formation of a new organisation to be known as the, Territorial Cadet Force. Units of the new force were to be administered by the Territorial Force Associations which had been impowered under the *Territorial and Reserve Forces Act* to establish or assist cadet battalions or corps.

The first regulations (provisional) for the TCF were issued as a Special Army Order dated, 21st May, 1910 and were to supersede any previously issued to cadet corps.

Under the heading "Regulations Governing The Formation, Organisation, And Administration Of Cadet Units By County Associations" the following was directed:-

The term "Cadet Unit" was to apply to Cadet Battalions, Cadet Companies, and all bodies of lads formed for the purpose of receiving instruction of a military nature. Units of the Boys Brigade, Church Lads Brigade and Jewish Lads Brigade, who had always worked closely with their local Army Volunteers or Territorials, were later also to apply for and gain recognition as Army Cadets.

The organisation of a cadet unit was not less than 30 cadets to one company. If the number of cadets in a unit exceeded 100, two companies could be formed with additional companies being raised upon the enlistment of every 100. Four or more companies were organised into battalions and the number of officers per unit was based upon the establishments set down for the Territorial force.

The authority to whom the Army Council delegated the power to grant official recognition to cadet units, or to cancel recognition already given, was the Territorial Force Association of the county in which the unit concerned had its headquarters.

The County Associations were responsible for seeing that all cadet units, which it had officially recognised, were efficiently organised and administered. They also had the power to raise new units, to nominate Cadet Officers for appointment and to issue rules, regulations and orders for the government of units under their control, subject to the approval of the War Office.

In order to gain recognition a cadet unit had to forward its application, accompanied by infomation as to its financial stability, direct to its local Territorial Force Association. In its application each unit had to undertake to make every effort to furnish recruits to the Territorial Force. Details of the number of companies into which it was proposed to organised the unit were required as were accounts of what facilities existed for drill, training and musketry. Applications also contained details of what, if any, unit of the Territorial Force the cadets preferred to be affiliated.

Associations, on granting official recognition of a cadet unit, were required to report their decision to the War Office together with details of size of unit, its title and headquarters and a list containing the names and ranks of officers.

Affiliation to a Territorial Force unit was granted by the officer commanding of the unit concerned. However the regulations required that where a cadet unit was affiliated to a non-infantry organisation only infantry training was permitted.

Details of cadet units granted recognition were published in Army Orders commencing with No 197 of 1910 and ending with No 29 of 1923. Army Orders were also to record any changes in organisation, amalgamations, disbandments and withdrawals of recognition by the Territorial Associations.

An official list of recognised cadet units, showing the Territorial Force units to which they are affiliated, their organisation and strength, and the names of their officers was published by the War Office on the 1st January of each year.

Subject to the approval of County Associations, the actual age at which enlistment into a cadet unit was permitted was decided by the rules of each unit. However cadets could not remain with their units, without the express sanction of the County Association, after they had reached the age at which enlistment into the Territorial Force became possible.

Cadets who enlisted into the Territorial Force within six months of leaving a recognised cadet unit were excused all, or part of, their recruits' drill. Cadet service could also count towards the grant of the Territorial Force Efficiency Medal, again providing that enlistment was within six months. No service before the age of fifteen was counted.

Gentlemen desirous of obtaining cadet commissions had to satisfy the County Association concerned that they were qualified to empart elementary military instruction to cadets, and that they were in every way suited to perform the duties of a cadet officer. Cadet commissions were issued on behalf of the King, by the Lieutenant of the County in which the officer's headquarters were situated. All ranks were honorary and junior to all Regular, Special Reserve or Territorial Force officers.

In order to obtain the grants given to Territorial Force Associations by the Government for their cadets, each unit was subject to annual inspection. Inspections were carried out by a Regular, Special Reserve or Territorial Force officer detailed by the General Officer Commanding-in-Chief of the command in which the cadet unit had its headquarters.

It was required by the Government that each cadet unit had to be entirely financially self-supporting and the Government Grant of £5 per company, annually, was to be used by the Territorial Force Association to meet the necessary expenses connected with the formation and administration of units. A reserve fund was also established by each association, to be used in any way thought likely to develop and assist the cadet organisations within the county.

In order for grants to be issued, the inspecting officer had to be satisfied that a cadet unit was so organised and conducted as to impart elementary military instruction in an efficient manner. That it conformed to the rules, regulations, and orders set down for its government, and that on the date of inspection each company had a strength of not less than 30 qualified cadets.

Such aid that did come from the Government in addition to the annual grant came in the form of permission to encamp on Government ground and the loan of equipment. The latter, however, required the cadets to provide all transport costs and be responsible for any loss or damage.

Recognised cadet units were also given permission to use Government ranges and War Department lands, as well as drill halls and buildings owned, leased or rented by County Associations.

Arms and ammunition was purchased from the Government by County Associations and distributed to cadet units either by sale, hire or free loan.

Revised editions of Cadet Regulations were issued in 1912, 1914 and 1921. In 1917 (Army Order 128) all units of the Church Lads Brigade, which hitherto had been unattached, became affiliated to the King's Royal Rifle Corps and in 1918 HRH The Prince of Wales became Colonel-in-Chief of the Cadet Force.

During the Great War interest in the Cadet Movement, both by the youth of the day and the Government, grew. Many new units were raised by battalions of the new Volunteer Force and by 1918 over two thousand companies had been officially recognised. Throughout the war cadets were frequently asked to patrol vulnerable points such as reservoirs or railway bridges and to act as air-raid buglers.

Also during the 1914-18 War a capitation grant of 6s.0d per cadet was introduced by the Government. This figure was divided; 5s.0d to the unit and 1s.0d. to the County Association.

In 1923 it was decided by the War Office to hand over complete control of the cadet forces to the Council of County Territorial Army Associations. With this all grants were cancelled except for a block payment of ₤750 annually.

THE REGISTER

This register represents a complete account of the cadet units recognised and recorded in Army Orders during the period 1910-1922 by the Territorial Force Associations of Gt. Britain.

Arranaged alphabetically each entry includes the title of the unit, its date of recognition and the TFA responsible for its administration. Records of Affiliation together with any changes in title, disbandments, amalgamations and alterations in establishment have also been noted.

Reference to Army Orders in which the above infomation was authorised is shown in the register as e.g. AO 302/16 (Army Order No 302 of 1916).

An index refering to the affiliation of cadet units is shown in Appendix "A". Here the code used is e.g. "A 33", indicating entry number 33 in the A section.

A

1. Abercard Territorial Cadet Company: Rec. 1.9.10 (Monmouth) (AO 258/10) and aff. to 2nd Bn. Monmouthshire Regt. Became part of the 1st Cadet Bn., Monmouthshire Regt. by AO 233/12.

2. Aberdare County School Cadet Corps: Rec. 26.4.19 (Glamorgan) (AO 251/19) and aff. to 5th Bn.,Welsh Regt. Disbanded by AO 265/22.

3. Aberdeen Cadet Battalion, 1st, The Boys Brigade: Formed by AO 398/21 and the amal. of the Aberdeen Cadet Company and the 2nd, 3rd, 4th, and 5th Aberdeen Companies of the Boys Brigade. Admin. by City of Aberdeen TFA.

4. Aberdeen Cadet Company, The Boys Brigade: Rec. 16.5.19 (City of Aberdeen) (AO 340/19). Became part of the 1st Aberdeen Cadet Battalion, The Boys Brigade by AO 398/21.

5. Aberdeen Cadet Companies, 2nd, 3rd, 4th and 5th, The Boys Brigade: Rec. 6.4.21 (City of Aberdeen) (AO 226/21). Became part of the 1st Aberdeen Cadet Battalion, The Boys Brigade by AO 398/21.

6. Aberdeen Cadet Company, 25th, The Boys Brigade: Rec. 1.10.22 (City of Aberdeen) (AO 401/22).

7. Aberdeen, City of, Cadet Battalion: Rec. 29.8.14 (City of Aberdeen) (AO 416/14). Aff. to 4th Bn. Gordon Highlanders by AO 69/19. Disbanded by AO 271/21.

8. Abergavenny Cadet Corps: Rec. 1.3.12 (Monmouth) (AO 143/12) and aff. to 3rd Bn. Monmouthshire Regt. Became part of the 1st Cadet Bn., Monmouthshire Regt. by AO 233/12.

9. Ackmar School (LCC) Cadet Company: See 2nd (Fulham) Bn. Imperial Cadet Corps.

10. Acton Cadet Company: Rec. 22.12.14 (Middlesex) (AO 79/15) and aff. to 10th Bn. Middlesex Regt. Became part of 4th Cadet Bn. Middlesex Regt. by AO 96/16.

11. Airdrie Cadet Company, 1st, The Boys Brigade: Rec. 17.12.20 (Lanark) (AO 25/21).

12. Alcester Cadet Company, Church Lads Brigade: Rec. 26.11.12 (Warwick) (AO 13/13). Absorbed into 2nd Worcester (Coventry) Cadet Bn. CLB by AO 381/15.

13. Aldershot Church Cadet Corps: Rec. 16.12.10 (Southampton) (AO 102/11) and aff. to Hampshire Brigade Company, ASC.

14. Aldershot County School Cadet Corps: Rec. 19.11.15 (Southampton) (AO 125/16) and aff. to 4th Bn. Hampshire Regt. Amal. with 1st Cadet Bn. of Hampshire and Peter Symonds School to form, 1/4th and 2/4th Hampshire Regt. Cadet Battalions by AO 307/18.

15. Alexandria Cadet Company, 2nd, The Boys Brigade: Rec. 10.1.22. (Dumbarton) (AO 265/22).

16. Allan Glen's School (Glasgow) Cadet Corps: Rec. 18.4.16 (City of Glasgow) (AO 302/16). Inc. to four companies by AO 378/18. Aff. to 5th Bn. Highland Light Infantry by AO 276/19. Reduced to two companies by AO 527/21.

17. Allan's School Cadet Unit: Rec. 2.5.13 (Northumberland) (AO 187/13) and aff. to 6th Bn. Northumberland Fusiliers.

18. Alleyn's Grammar School (Stone) Cadet Corps: Rec. 28.9.18 (Stafford) (AO 373/18) and aff. to 1st Volunteer Bn. North Staffordshire Regt.

19. Alleyn's School Cadet Corps: Rec. 14.7.15 (County of London) (AO 343/15) and aff. to 21st Bn. London Regt. Inc. to twelve companies by AO 310/22.

20. All Saints', Shrewsbury Cadet Company, Church Lads Brigade: Rec. 10.2.18 (Shropshire) (AO 173/18). Redes. **All Saints' and St. Giles, Shrewsbury** by AO 251/19.

21. All Soul's Cadet Company, Weaste Salford Diocesan Catholic Boys Brigade: Rec. 9.5.19 (East Lancs) (AO 251/19). Absorbed into 7th Cadet Bn. Salford Diocesan Catholic Boys Brigade by A.O. 340/19.

22. Almondbury Grammar School Cadet Corps: Rec. 1.10.15 (West Yorks) (AO 457/15) and aff. to 5th Bn. Duke of Wellington's Regt.

23. Alsop High School Cadet Corps: Rec. 24.3.19 (West Lancs) (AO 219/19). Redes. **"B" Company (Alsop High School), 5th Cadet Bn. King's Liverpool Regt.** by AO 95/22.

24. Alyth Cadet Company, 1st, The Boys Brigade: Rec. 1.11.22 (Perth) (AO 435/22).

25. Archbishop Holgate's Grammar School Cadet Corps: Rec. 1.9.15 (West Yorks) (AO 381/15) and aff. to 5th Bn. West Yorkshire Regt.

26. Archbishop Temple's School Cadet Corps: Rec. 23.4.11 (City of London) (AO 161/11). Rec. withdrawn by AO 49/13.

27. Argyll and Sutherland Highlanders, 1st Cadet Company, 5th Bn.: See 1/1st Bn. Renfrewshire Volunteer Regt.

28. Argyll and Sutherland Highlanders, 1st (Dumbartonshire) Cadet Bn: Rec. 1.5.17 (Dumbarton) (AO 275/17) and aff. to 9th Bn. Inc. to eight companies by AO 111/18.

29. Armstrong-Whitworth Walker Cadet Company, Northumberland Fusiliers: Rec. 21.8.20 (Northumberland) (AO 25/21) and aff. to 5th Bn.

30. Arnold House (Llanddulas) Cadet Corps: Rec. 1.10.15 (Denbigh) (AO 430/15). Disbanded by AO 323/21.

31. Arnold House School Cadet Corps: Rec. 10.11.10 (West Lancs) (AO 11/11) and aff. to 4th Bn. North Lancs. Regt.

32. Arrol-Johnston Cadet Corps: Rec. 16.7.17 (Dumfries) (AO 360/17) and aff. to 5th Bn. King's Own Scottish Borderers.

33. Artillery, Royal, No1 Cadet Corps, Beccles: Rec. 22.11.10 (Suffolk) (AO 11/11) and aff. to 3rd East Anglian (Howitzer) Brigade, RFA.

34. Artists Rifles Cadet Corps: Rec. 11.2.18 (County of London) (AO 149/18) and aff. to 28th Bn. London Regt. Disbanded by AO 116/20.

35. Ashford Grammar School Cadet Corps: Rec. 2.10.13 (Kent) (AO 373/13). Aff. to Royal East Kent Yeomanry by AO 65/17. Absorbed into Kent Public Secondary Schools Cadet Bn. by AO 137/19.

36. Ashville College (Harrogate) Cadet Corps: Rec. 28.9.16 (West Yorks) (AO 375/16) and aff. to 5th Bn. West Yorkshire Regt. Disbanded by AO 156/20.

37. Aske's Hatcham School Cadet Corps: Rec. 10.11.14 (City of London) (AO 79/15) and aff. to 21st Bn. London Regt.

38. Aspatria Company, Church Lads Brigade: See Aspatria and Christ Church Carlisle Company, CLB.

39. Aspatria and Christ Church, Carlisle Company, Church Lads Brigade: Rec. 28.11.11 (Cumberland) (AO 75/12). Rec. withdrawn and the company divided into two units, **Aspatria Company** and **Christ Church, Carlisle Company** by AO 187/13. Christ Church disbanded by AO 401/22.

40. Austin Works Cadet Corps: Rec. 24.5.18 (Worcester) (AO 209/18) and aff. to Royal Engineers Signal Service (TF).

41. Axminster Cadet Company, Church Lads Brigade: Rec. 11.12.12 (Devon) (AO 13/13). Disbanded 1.12.15 (AO 96/16).

42. Aylesbury Grammar School Cadet Corps: Rec. 21.9.14 (Bucks) (AO 451/14) and aff. to Buckinghamshire Bn., Oxfordshire and Buckinghamshire Light Infantry.

43. Aylwin College Cadet Company: Rec. 27.4.17 (Westmoreland) (AO 275/17) and aff. to 4th Bn. Border Regt. Inc. to two companies by AO 276/19.

44. Ayr Cadet Battalion, The Boys Brigade: Rec. 7.5.18 (Ayr) (AO 240/18).

45. Ayrshire Dockyard Company, 1st Cadet Bn., Royal Scots Fusiliers: Rec. 1.9.19 (Ayr) (AO 419/19) and aff. to 4th Bn.

B

1. Bablake School (Coventry) Cadet Company: Rec. 4.3.14 (Warwick) (AO 104/14) and aff. to 7th Bn. Royal Warwickshire Regt. Absorbed into the 3rd Cadet Bn. Royal Warwickshire Regt. by AO 261/15.

2. Baine's Grammar School Cadet Corps: Rec. 28.6.20 (West Lancs) (AO 317/20) and aff. to 5th Bn. King's Own Royal Lancaster Regt.

3. Balham and Upper Tooting Cadet Company: See Upper Tooting High School.

4. Bancroft's School Cadet Company: Formed by AO 128/17 and added to 5th (Schools) Cadet Bn. Essex Regt. In AO 184/21 the school is shown as having been removed from the 5th Cadet Bn. and recognised, 15.1.21 as an independent unit aff. to 4th Bn. Essex Regt. Admin. by Essex TFA.

5. Bargeddie Cadets, 1st, The Boys Brigade: Rec. 19.11.20 (Lanark) (AO 555/20).

6. Barking Cadet Corps: Rec. 16.6.17 (Essex) (AO 275/17) and aff. to 4th Bn. Essex Regt. Inc. to two companies by AO 240/18.

7. Barrow Secondary School Cadet Corps: Rec. 16.3.18 (West Lancs) (AO 149/18) and aff. to 4th Bn. King's Own Royal Lancaster Regt.

8. Barry County School Cadet Corps: Rec. 23.3.17 (Glamorgan) (AO 168/17) and aff. to Glamorgan (Fortress) Royal Engineers. Disbanded by AO 156/20.

9. Basingstoke and Eastrop Cadet Corps: Rec. 28.4.11 (Southampton) (AO 161/11) and aff. to 4th Bn. Hampshire Regt.

10. Bath and Wells Cadet Battalion, 1st, Church Lads Brigade: Rec. 15.8.12 (Somerset) (AO 290/12). Inc. to seven companies by AO 251/19. Inc. to eight companies by AO 340/19. Inc. to nine companies by AO 24/20. Inc. to ten companies by AO 61/20.

11. Bath and Wells Cadet Battalion. 2nd, Church Lads Brigade: Rec. 15.8.12 (Somerset) (AO 260/12). Reduced to one company by AO 24/20.

12. Bath and Wells Cadet Corps, 3rd, Church Lads Brigade: Rec. 4.2.15 (Somerset) (AO 109/15). Reduced to one company by AO 340/19. Disbanded by AO 61/20.

13. Bath and Wells Cadet Corps, 4th, Church Lads brigade: Rec. 20.3.13 (Somerset) (AO 121/13).

14. Batley Company, 4th, The Boys Brigade Cadets: Rec. 7.7.19 (West Yorks) (AO 276/19).

15. Battersea Cadet Corps, 1st Battalion: See 1st Cadet Bn., 14th London Volunteer Regt.

16. Battersea Grammar School Cadet Corps: Rec. 1.12.14 (County of London) (AO 41/15). Inc. to eight companies by AO 25/21. Reduced to four companies by AO 310/22.

17. Beardmore Cadet Corps: Rec. 4.2.18 (City of Glasgow) (AO 149/18) and aff. to 7th Bn. Highland Light Infantry. Reduced to two companies by AO 527/21.

18. Beaumaris Grammar School Cadet Corps: Rec. 25.8.16 (Anglesea) (AO 335/16). Disbanded by AO 24/20.

19. Bedford Park Cadet Company: Rec. 18.9.11 (Middlesex) (AO 316/11) and aff. to 10th Bn. Middlesex Regt. Rec. withdrawn by AO 187/13. Re-rec by AO 511/14. Became part of 4th Cadet Bn. Middlesex Regt. by AO 96/16.

20. Berkshire Regt.,1st and 2nd Cadet Companies, 4th Battalion: 1st Company rec. 7.3.14 (AO 104/14). 2nd Company formed 1.7.15. Both companies admin. by Berkshire TFA. Redes. **Maidenhead Cadet Companies, 4th Bn. Royal Berkshire Regt.** by AO 302/15.

21. Beverley Cadet Company, 1st, The Boys Brigade: Rec. 26.3.18 (East Yorks) (AO 173/18). Disbanded by AO 72/21.

22. Beverley Grammar School Cadet Corps: Rec. 13.11.16 (East Yorks) (AO 406/16). Aff. to 4th Bn. East Yorkshire Regt. by A.O. 255/20.

23. Beccles Cadets: See Royal Artillery, No 1 Cadet Battalion.

24. Bideford Cadet Company, Church Lads Brigade: Rec. 22.7.14 (Devon) (AO 416/14).

25. Birkenhead Cadet Company, 1st, The Boys Brigade: Rec. 8.5.18 (Chester) (AO 240/18).

26. Birkenhead Cadet Company, 4th, The Boys Brigade: Rec. 11.2.18 (Chester) (AO 149/18).

27. Birkenhead Cadet corps, 1st: Rec. 5.6.13 (Chester) (AO 235/13) and aff. to 4th Bn. Cheshire Regt. Rec. withdrawn by AO 251/19.

28. Birkenhead School Cadet Corps: See 1st Oxton (Birkenhead School) Cadet Corps.

29. Birmingham Cadet Battalion, Church Lads Brigade: Rec. 28.7.13 (Warwick) (AO 337/13). Inc. to eight companies by AO 342/18.

30. Birmingham Cadet Battalion, 3rd, Church Lads Brigade: Rec. 3.12.18 (Stafford) (AO 31/19). Amal. with Holy Trinity, Wilnecote Cadet Company, CLB by AO 31/19. Transfered to the Warwick TFA by AO 219/19. Redes. **2nd Coventry Cadet Bn. CLB** by AO 317/20. Amal. with Holy Trinity cancelled by AO 527/21.

31. Birmingham Cadet Company, 1st, Jewish Lads Brigade: Rec. 5.5.15 (Warwick) (AO 261/15). Inc. to two companies and designated **Birmingham Cadet Corps, JLB** by AO 209/18.

32. Biscot Company, Church Lads Brigade Cadets: Rec. 12.7.18 (Bedford) (AO 31/19).

33. Bishop Wordsworth's School Cadet Corps: Rec. 4.3.17 (Wilts) (AO 168/17). Aff. to 4th Bn. Wiltshire Regt. by AO 275/17.

34. Bishop's Stortford College Cadet Company: See 5th Hertfordshire Cadets.

35. Blairgowrie Company, "G", 1st Perthshire Cadet Battalion, The Boys Brigade: Rec. 16.3.21 (Perth) (AO 184/21).

36. Bletchingley and Godstone Cadet Corps: Rec. 15.7.18 (Surrey) (AO 307/18) and aff. to 2nd Volunteer Bn. Royal West Surrey Regt. Became part of 4th Cadet Bn. Royal West Surrey Regt. by AO 103/19).

37. Blyth Shipbuilding and Drydock Cadet Detachment, Northumberland Fusiliers: Rec. 28.4.21 (Northumberland) (AO 323/21) and aff. to 72nd (Northumbrian) Brigade, RFA.

38. Bolton Boys Brigade, 1st Cadet Battalion: Rec. 11.2.21 (East Lancs) (AO 184/21). Reduced to six companies by AO 95/22.

39. Bolton Grammar School Cadet Corps: Rec. 11.3.15 (West Lancs) (AO 225/15). Aff. to 5th Bn. Loyal North Lancashire Regt. by AO 275/17. Redes. **Bolton School Cadet Corps** by AO 276/19.

40. Bolton School Cadet Corps: See Bolton Grammar School.

41. Bolton YMCA Cadet Corps: Rec. 22.10.20 (West Lancs) (AO 514/20) and aff. to 5th Bn. Loyal North Lancashire Regt. Inc. to two companies by AO 29/23.

42. Borden Grammar School (Sittingbourne) Cadet Corps: Rec. 24.11.16 (Kent) (AO 65/17) and aff. to 4th Bn. East Kent Regt. Absorbed into Kent Public Secondary Schools Cadet Battalion by AO 137/19.

43. Borough Polytechnic Cadet Corps: Rec. 26.9.16 (County of London) (AO 375/16) and aff. to 24th Bn. London Regt. Disbanded by AO 29/23.

44. Bournemouth Cadet Company, 3rd, The Boys Brigade: Rec. 5.7.19 (Southampton) (AO 419/19).

45. Bourton Cadet Company, 1st, The Boys Brigade: Rec. 20.4.18 (Dorset) (AO 173/18). Disbanded by AO 61/20.

46. Bowling Boys Brigade Cadet Corps: Rec. 18.1.21 (Dumbarton) (AO 72/21).

47. Boxgrove School Cadet Corps: Rec. 3.6.18 (Surrey) (AO 240/18) and aff. to 3rd Volunteer Bn. Royal West Surrey Regt. Transferred to 5th Bn. by AO 116/20.

48. Boys Brigade Cadet Battalion, Plymouth: Rec. 19.6.18 (Devon) (AO 307/18).

49. Boys Brigade Cadets (10th Hertfordshire), Barnet: Rec. 17.12.17 (Hertford) (AO 111/18). Inc. to three companies by AO 419/19.

50. Boys Scottish Cadet Company: Rec. 24.3.19 (West Lancs) (AO 219/19).

51. Bradford Battalion, Catholic Boys Brigade: Rec. 10.6.13 (West Yorks) (AO 274/13). Disbanded by AO 156/20.

52. Bradford Cadet Battalion, 1st Church Lads Brigade: See 2nd Ripon Cadet Bn. CLB.

53. Bradford Postal Telegraph Messengers Cadet Corps: Rec. 1.4.10 (West Yorks) (AO 225/10) and aff. to 6th Bn. West Yorkshire Regt.

54. Bradford Volunteer Cadet Battalion: Rec. 8.7.18 (West Yorks) (AO 307/18) and aff. to Bradford Group, West Riding Volunteers. Transfered to 6th Bn. West Yorkshire Regt. by AO 116/20.

55. Bradwell Training School Cadet Corps: Rec. 7.11.17 (Chester) (AO 51/18) and aff. to 4th Bn. Cheshire Volunteer Regt. Aff. transfered to 7th Bn. Cheshire Regt. by AO 116/20.

56. Braintree and Bocking Cadet Company: Rec. 29.6.16 (Essex) (AO 262/16) and aff. to 5th Bn. Essex Regt. Absorbed into 8th Cadet Bn. Essex Regt. by AO 51/18.

57. Braintree County High School Cadets: Rec. 17.12.15 (Essex) (AO 62/16) and aff. to 5th Bn. Essex Regt.

58. Brecknell, Munro and Rodgers Cadet Engineer Field Company: Rec. 23.9.18 (Gloucester) (AO 31/19) and aff. to Bristol Volunteer Battalion. Disbanded by AO 251/19.

59. Brecon Cadet Company, Church Lads Brigade: Rec. 1.9.15 (Brecknock) (AO 381/15).

60. Brentwood Cadets: See Sir Anthony Browne's School.

61. Brentwood Company, 1st, The Boys Brigade Cadets: Rec. 1.10.19 (Essex) (AO 371/20).

62. Bridgend County School Cadet Corps: Rec. 29.6.15 (Glamorgan) (AO 302/15) and aff. to 6th Bn. Welsh Regt. Disbanded by AO 156/20.

63. Bridgnorth Cadet Corps: Rec. 1.5.12 (Shropshire) (AO 177/12) and aff. to 4th Bn. Shropshire Light Infantry.

64. Brierfield Cadet Company, Church Lads Brigade: Rec. 4.12.14 (East Lancs) (AO 79/15).

65. Brierley Hill Cadet Corps: Rec. 15.7.10 (Stafford) (AO 197/10) and aff. to 6th Bn. South Staffordshire Regt. Disbanded by AO 65/17.

66. Brightlingsea (Cadet) Company, 1st, The Boys Brigade: Rec. 14.6.22 (Essex) (AO 265/22).

67. Brighton Brigade, Sussex Cadets: Rec. 28.2.14 (Sussex) (AO 188/14) and aff. to 1st Home Counties Brigade, RFA. Redes. **1st, 2nd and 3rd Cadet Regiments, Sussex Yeomanry** by AO 23/16. 1st and 3rd Regts. disbanded by AO 514/20. 2nd Regt. disbanded by AO 527/21.

68. Brighton (Cadet) Company, 2nd, The Boys Brigade: Rec. 22.5.22 (Sussex) (AO 401/22).

69. Brighton (Cadet) Company, 3rd, The Boys Brigade: Rec. 4.3.21 (Sussex) (AO 226/21).

70. Brighton Cadet Corps, 4th, The Boys Brigade (Hove): Rec. 27.7.21 (Sussex) (AO 493/21).

71. Brighton (Cadet) Company, 8th, The Boys Brigade: Rec. 26.5.21 (Sussex) (AO 398/21).

72. Brighton (Cadet) Company, 10th, The Boys Brigade: Rec. 26.5.21 (Sussex) (AO 398/21).

73. Brighton (Cadet) Company, 21st, The Boys Brigade: Rec. 27.7.21 (Sussex) (AO 493/21).

74. Brighton (Cadet) Company, 26th, The Boys Brigade: Rec. 4.3.21 (Sussex) (AO 226/21).

75. Brighton, Hove and Sussex Grammar School Cadet Corps: Rec. 16.3.15 (Sussex) (AO 225/15) and aff. to 4th Bn. Royal Sussex Regt.

76. Brighton Preparatory School Cadet Corps: Rec. 10.10.10 (Sussex) (AO 11/11) and aff. to 4th Bn. Royal Sussex Regt. Disbanded 14.12.14 (AO 41/15). Disbandment cancelled by AO 109/15. Disbanded by AO 116/20.

77. Brighton Secondary and Technical Schools Cadet Corps: Rec. 1.2.15 (Sussex) (AO 225/15) and aff. to Home Counties Divisional Royal Engineers. Inc. to three companies by AO 69/19). Disbanded by AO 365/21).

78. Brigg Grammar School Cadet corps: Rec. 23.5.16 (Lincoln) (AO 229/16) and aff. to 5th Bn. Lincolnshire Regt.

79. Brimscombe Polytechnic Cadet Corps: Rec. 20.3.16 (Gloucester) (AO 125/16) and aff. to 5th Bn. Gloucestershire Regt.

80. Bristol Cadet Battalion, 1st, Church Lads Brigade: See 2nd Gloucester Cadet Bn. CLB.

81. Bristol Cadet Battalion, 2nd, Church Lads Brigade: Rec. 20.12.20 (Gloucester) (AO 25/21). Disbanded by AO 401/22.

82. Bristol Company, 26th, The Boys Brigade: Rec. 18.12.17 (Gloucester) (AO 111/18).

83. Broadwater Cadet Corps: See Broadwater Scouting Corps.

84. Broadwater Scouting Corps: Rec. 22.6.12 (County of London) (AO 260/12). Redes. **Broadwater Cadet Corps** by AO 373/13. Disbanded by AO 219/19.

85. Brockley Secondary School Cadet Corps: Rec. 28.6.18 (County of London) (AO 307/18) and aff. to 16th Bn. London Regt.

86. Bromley School Cadet Corps: Rec. 28.1.15 (Kent) (AO 96/16). Absorbed into Kent Public Secondary Schools Cadet Bn. by AO 137/19.

87. Bromsgrove Secondary School Cadet Company: Rec. 26.6.15 (Worcester) (AO 302/15) and aff. to 8th Bn. Worcestershire Regt. Became part of **Worcestershire Cadet Battalion** by AO 188/16.

88. Brondesbury College Cadet Corps: Rec. 15.3.15 (Middlesex) (AO 139/15) and aff. to 9th Bn. Middlesex Regt. Became part of 3rd Cadet Bn. Middlesex Regt. by AO 96/16.

89. Broomfield Cadet Company: Rec. 28.4.16 (Essex) (AO 188/16) and aff. to 5th Bn. Essex Regt. Absorbed into 8th Cadet Bn. Essex Regt. by AO 51/18.

90. Broomsleigh Street School (LCC) Cadet Company: Rec. 26.11.15 (City of London) (AO 96/16). Redes. **Broomsleigh Street Detachment, 1st Cadet Bn. Royal Fusiliers** by AO 484/22.

91. Broughton Lads Brigade: Rec. 4.10.12 (East Lancs) (AO 343/12) and aff. to 7th Bn. Lancashire Fusiliers. Redes. **1st Cadet Company, 8th Bn. Lancashire Fusiliers** by AO 104/14. Disbanded 29.1.15 (AO 109/15).

92. Brynmawr and Beauford Cadet Company: See 3rd Cadet Bn. Monmouthshire Regt.

93. Brynmawr Cadet Company, Church Lads Brigade: Rec. 7.3.21 (Brecknock) (AO 184/21).

94. Burford Grammar School Cadet Corps: Rec. 30.9.10 (Oxford) (AO 281/10) and aff. to 4th Bn. Oxfordshire and Buckinghamshire Light Infantry.

95. Burnley Cadet Company, 1st: Rec. 27.8.20 (East Lancs) (AO 459/20) and aff. to 5th Bn. East Lancashire Regt.

96. Burnley Cadet Corps: Rec. 12.4.18 (East Lancs) (AO 173/18) and aff. to 1/11th Lancashire Volunteer Regt. Disbanded by AO 116/20.

97. Burntisland Cadet Company, 1st, The Boys Brigade: Rec. 21.10.21 (Fife) (AO 493/21).

98. Burton-on-Trent Cadet Corps: Rec. 22.4.18 (Stafford) (AO 173/18) and aff. to 2nd Bn. Staffordshire Volunteer Regt. Disbanded by AO 116/20.

99. Burton-on-Trent Grammar School Cadet Corps: Rec. 26.12.16 (Stafford) (AO 65/17). Absorbed into 1st Secondary School Cadet Bn. (Staffordshire Regt.) by AO 373/18.

100. Buxton College Cadet Corps: Rec. 18.10.15 (Derby) (AO 457/15). Absorbed into Derbyshire Schools Cadet Bn. by AO 219/19.

C

1. Cadet Field Ambulance, 1st: Rec. 5.3.18 (East Yorks) (AO 173/18) and aff. to 1st East Yorks Volunteer Field Ambulance. Redes. **East Riding Cadet Field Ambulance** and aff. to 3rd Northumbrian Field Ambulance RAMC by AO 255/20.

2. Cadet Norfolk Artillery: Rec. 12.4.13 (Norfolk) (AO 187/13) and aff. to 1st East Anglian Brigade RFA. Absorbed 1st Norfolk Volunteer Cadet Corps and inc. to nine companies 16.7.19 (AO 419/19).

3. Caistor Grammar School Cadet Company: Rec. 18.11.17 (Lincoln) (AO 111/18). Aff. to 5th Bn. Lincolnshire Regt. by AO 72/21.

4. Calder Farm Cadet Corps: Rec. 22.8.18 (West Yorks) (AO 307/18).

5. Caldicot Cadet Company: See 1st Cadet Bn. Monmouthshire Regt.

6. Caldy Grange Grammar School Cadet Corps: Rec. 11.11.15 (Chester) (AO 23/16) and aff. to 4th Bn. Cheshire Regt. Inc. to two companies by AO 275/17. Reduced to one company by AO 435/22.

7. Cambridge Company, 1st, The Boys Brigade Cadets: Rec. 6.10.17 (Cambs and Ely) (AO 360/17).

8. Cambridge Company, 5th, The Boys Brigade Cadets: Rec. 6.10.17 (Cambs and Ely) (AO 360/17).

9. Cambridge Scientific Instrument Co. Ltd. Cadet Signal Company, Royal Engineers: Rec. 2.11.18 (Cambs and Ely) (AO 31/19). Disbanded by AO 61/20.

10. Camelon Company, 1st, Boys Brigade Cadets: Rec. 2.5.22 (Stirling) (AO 265/22).

11. Cameronians (Scottish Rifles), 5th Bn. Cadet Battalion: See 3rd City of Glasgow Cadet Bn.

12. Campbeltown Grammar School Cadet Corps: Rec. 3.7.18 (Argyll) (AO 307/18) and aff. to 1st Bn. Argyllshire Volunteer Regt. Transferred to 8th Bn. Argyll and Sutherland Highlanders by AO 116/20.

13. Campden Grammar School Cadet Corps: Rec. 20.12.15 (Gloucester) (AO 62/16) and aff. to 5th Bn. Gloucestershire Regt. Transferred to Worcester TFA by AO 452/21. Transferred to 8th Bn. Worcestershire Regt. by AO 493/21.

14. Campsie Cadet Company: Rec. 4.9.17 (Stirling) (AO 360/17) and aff. to 1st Bn. Stirlingshire Volunteer Regt. Became part of 1st Stirlingshire Cadet Bn. by AO 31/19.

15. Canterbury Cadet Battalion, 1st, Church Lads Brigade: Rec. 8.7.12 (Surrey) (AO 260/12).

16. Canterbury Cadet Battalion, 2nd, Church Lads Brigade: Rec. 21.11.11 (Kent) (AO 177/12). Absorbed Christ Church, Folkestone Cadets, CLB by AO 96/16.

17. Cargo Fleet Iron Company Cadet Corps: Rec. 21.2.18 (North Yorks) (AO 149/18) and aff. to 1/1st Bn. North Riding Volunteer Regt. Disbanded by AO 103/19.

18. Carlisle Battalion, The Boys Brigade: Rec. 29.8.17 (Cumberland) (AO 360/17).

19. Carlisle Cadet Battalion, No 7, The Boys Brigade: Rec. 31.7.20 (Cumberland) (AO 514/20) and aff. to 4th Bn. Border Regt. Aff. cancelled by AO 25/21.

20. Carlisle Grammar School Cadet Companies: Rec. 11.12.17 (Cumberland) (AO 11/18) and aff. to 1/1st Bn. Cumberland Volunteer Regt. Reduced to one company by AO 24/20. Aff. transfered to 4th Bn. Border Regt. by AO 116/20. Disbanded by AO 493/21.

21. Carnarvon County School Cadet Corps: Rec. 1.12.15 (Carnarvon) (AO 23/16). Disbanded by AO 340/19).

22. Carnarvon Town Cadet Corps: Rec. 1.8.19 (Carnarvon) (AO 340/19) and aff. to 6th Bn. Roal Welsh Fusiliers.

23. Castle Mills Cadet Battalion: Rec. 1.4.18 (City of Edinburgh) (AO 173/18) and aff. to Royal Scots. Reduced to one company by AO 401/22.

24. Caterham Cadet Corps: Rec. 3.12.17 (Surrey) (AO 111/18) and aff. to 4th Bn. Royal West Surrey Regt. Became part of 4th Cadet Bn. Royal West Surrey Regt. by AO 103/19.

25. Catholic Cadets: See Westminster Bn. Catholic Boys Brigade.

26. Cavendish School (Matlock) Cadet Corps: Rec. 12.6.16 (Derby) (AO 229/16). Aff. to 6th Bn. Notts and Derby Regt. by AO 335/16. Disbanded by AO 69/19).

27. Chapelhall Cadet Company, 1st, The Boys Brigade: Rec. 22.4.21 (Lanark) (AO 226/21).

28. Chard School Cadet Corps: Rec. 1.3.22 (Somerset) (AO 265/22) and aff. to 5th Bn. Somerset Light Infantry.

29. Chatham Cadet Company, 1st, Royal Marine Light Infantry: Rec. 1.4.12 (Kent) (AO 207/12) and aff. to 5th Bn. Royal West Kent Regt.

30. Chatham Company, Catholic Boys Brigade: Rec. 27.10.13 (Kent) (AO 10/14). Disbanded by AO 219/19.

31. Chatham House (Ramsgate) Cadet Corps: Rec. 1.5.11 (Kent) (AO 220/11) and aff. to 4th Bn. East Kent Regt. Placed into "temporary abeyance" by AO 360/17.

32. Chelmsford Cadet Battalions, 1st, 2nd and 3rd, Church Lads Brigade: See 1st, 4th and 5th St. Albans Battalions, CLB.

33. Chelmsford, King Edward VI, School Cadet Corps: Rec. 29.6.10 (Essex) (AO 197/10) and aff. to 5th Bn. Essex Regt. Inc. to two companies by AO 419/19. Reduced to one company by AO 150/22.

34. Cheltenham Cadet Corps: Rec. 17.12.17 (Gloucester) (AO 111/18) and aff. to 3rd Bn. Gloucestershire Volunteer Regt. Disbanded by AO 61/20.

35. Cheltenham Grammar School Cadet Corps: Rec. 18.9.16 (Gloucester) (AO 406/16) and aff. to 5th Bn. Gloucestershire Regt. Inc. to three companies by AO 69/19. Disbanded by AO 323/21.

36. Chepstow Territorial Cadet Company: Rec. 16.7.10 (Monmouth) (AO 197/10) and aff. to 1st Bn. Monmouthshire Regt. Became part of 1st Cadet Bn. Monmouthshire Regt. by AO 233/12.

37. Cheshire Regt., 1st Territorial Cadet Battalion: Rec. 29.6.10 (Chester) (AO 197/10) and aff. to 6th Bn. Cheshire Regt. Redes. **1st Cheshire Royal Garrison Artillery Cadet Corps** and aff. to 6th Cheshire and Shropshire Medium Brigade RGA by AO 493/21.

38. Cheshire RGA, 1st, Cadet Corps: See 1st Territorial Cadet Bn. Cheshire Regt.

39. Cheshire, Sons of Empire Cadet Corps, 1st: Rec. 14.3.16 (Chester) (AO 160/16). Rec. withdrawn by AO 137/19).

40. Chester Cadet Corps, 1st, Church Lads Brigade: Rec. 7.5.15 (Cheshire) (AO 261/15). Redes. **1st Chester Cadet Bn. CLB** by AO 23/16.

41. Chester Cadet Battalion, 3rd, Church Lads Brigade: Rec. 27.4.12 (Chester) (AO 177/12).

42. Chester Cadet Battalion, 4th, Church Lads Brigade: Rec. 26.4.21 (Chester) (AO 226/21). Reduced to three companies by AO 401/22.

43. Chester Cadet Battalion, 6th, Church Lads Brigade: Rec. 19.8.13 (Chester) (AO 337/13).

44. Chester Cadet Battalion, 7th, Church Lads Brigade: Rec. 30.10.14 (Chester) (AO 511/14). Inc. to six companies by AO 373/18.

45. Chesterfield Grammar School Cadet Corps: Rec. 13.12.15 (Derby) (AO 62/16) and aff. to 6th Bn. notts and Derby Regt. Absorbed into the Derbyshire Schools Cadet Bn. by AO 219/19.

46. Chester-le-Street Parish Church Cadet Company: Rec. 9.4.18 (Durham) (AO 342/18) and aff. to 8th Bn. Durham L.I. Disbanded by AO 371/20.

47. Chichester Cadet Battalion, 1st, Church Lads Brigade: Rec. 26.5.14 (Sussex) (AO 416/14). Reduced to three companies by AO 61/20.

48. Chichester Cadet Battalion, 2nd, Church Lads Brigade: Rec. 8.1.12 (Sussex) (AO 177/12). Absorbed No 1 Cadet Company, 3rd Bn. Sussex Volunteer Regt. 21.4.19 (AO 251/19). Reduced to four companies by AO 452/21.

49. Chichester Cadet Battalion, 3rd, Church Lads Brigade: Rec. 9.10.11 (Sussex) (AO 75/12) and aff. to 4th Bn. Royal Sussex Regt. Inc. to five companies by AO 61/20. Reduced to four companies by AO 150/22.

50. Chichester Cadet Corps, 4th, Church Lads Brigade: Rec. 8.7.12 (Sussex) (AO 260/12). Reduced to three companies by AO 150/22.

51. Chichester Cadet Battalion. 5th, Church Lads Brigade: Rec. 8.1.12 (Sussex) (AO 177/12). Disbanded by AO 111/18.

52. Chorley Wood Company: See 1st Hertfordshire Cadets.

53. Christchurch Cadet Company: Rec. 1.6.19 (Southampton) (AO 276/19) and aff. to 7th Bn. Hampshire Regt.

54. Christ Church Cadet Corps: Rec. 1.6.22 (Sussex) (AO 310/22) and aff. to 230 (Sussex) Battery, 58th Home Counties Brigade, RFA.

55. Christ Church, Carlisle Cadet Company, Church Lads Brigade: See Aspatria and Christ Church, Carlisle Company, CLB.

56. Christ Church, Folkestone Cadets, Church Lads Brigade Naval Section: Rec. 14.4.15 (Kent) (AO 225/15). Absorbed into 2nd Canterbury Cadet Bn. CLB by AO 125/16.

57. Christ Church, West Bromwich Cadet Company, Church Lads Brigade: Rec. 20.11.16 (Stafford) (AO 406/16). Disbanded by AO 61/20.

58. Christ College (Brecon) Cadet Corps: Rec. 7.4.16 (Brecknock) (AO 160/16) and aff. to Brecknockshire Bn., South Wales Borderers. Disbanded by AO 452/21.

59. Christ's College Cadet Company: Rec. 11.12.11 (Middlesex) (AO 75/12) and aff. to 7th Bn. Middlesex Regt. Became part of 1st Cadet Bn. Middlesex Regt. by AO 96/16.

60. Church Institute School Cadet Corps: Rec. 15.2.18 (East Lancs) (AO 149/18). Rec. withdrawn by AO 493/21.

61. Church Loyalty Guards: See 1st Cadet Bn. of Cornwall.

62. Church of England Men's Society Company: See 3rd Lincoln Cadet Bn.

63. Church of the Ascension Cadet Corps, Victoria Docks ("E" Company, 1st Cadet Battalion, Essex Regt.): Rec. 28.9.10 (Essex) (AO 281/10) and aff. to 6th Bn. Essex Regt. Became part of 1st Cadet Bn. Essex Regt. by AO 65/11.

64. Cinque Ports Cadet Corps, 1st: Rec. 11.5.14 (Sussex) (AO 416/14) and aff. to 5th Bn. Royal Sussex Regt. Disbanded 11.11.16 (AO 360/17).

65. Cinque Ports (Fortress) Royal Engineers, 1st Cadet Company: Rec. 8.10.15 (Kent) (AO 430/15). Absorbed into Kent Public Secondary Schools Cadet Battalion by AO 137/19.

66. Cirencester Cadet Company, 1st, The Boys Brigade: Rec. 16.6.19 (Gloucester) (AO 276/19). Rec. withdrawn by AO 435/22.

67. Civil Service Cadet Corps: Rec. 2.2.11 (County of London) (AO 102/11) and aff. to 15th Bn. London Regt. Redes. **2nd (Civil Service) Cadet Battalion, London Regt.** in 1912. Inc. to six companies by AO 340/19. Disbanded by AO 116/20.

68. Clark's College (Southend-on-Sea) Cadet Corps: Rec. 11.4.17 (Essex) (AO 168/17) and aff. to 6th Bn. Essex Regt. Amal. with Highfield College Cadets and designated **9th Cadet Bn., Essex Regt.** by AO 111/18.

69. Clementswood Cadets: Rec. 10.2.15 (Essex) (AO 225/15) and aff. to 4th Bn. Essex Regt. Rec. withdrawn 14.11.17 (AO 111/18).

70. Cockburn High School (Hunslet) Cadet Corps: Rec. 18.5.15 (West Yorks) (AO 343/15). Aff. to 7th Bn. West Yorkshire Regt. by AO 430/15. Disbanded by AO 435/22.

71. Cockington Cadet Company, Church Lads Brigade: Rec. 3.8.15 (Devon) (AO 343/15). Disbanded by AO 251/19.

72. Colchester Company, 1st, The Boys Brigade Cadets: Rec. 21.6.19 (Essex) (AO 276/19).

73. Colchester Royal Grammar School Cadets: Rec. 25.10.11 (Essex) (AO 347/11) and aff. to 5th Bn. Essex Regt.

74. Coldhurst, Oldham Cadet Corps, 1st: Rec. 5.5.11 (East Lancs) (AO 161/11) and aff. to 10th Bn. Manchester Regt. Redes. **2nd Cadet Bn. Manchester Regt.** by AO 11/12. Reduced to two companies by AO 401/22.

75. Collegiate School Cadet Company, Hastings: Rec. 10.4.11 (Sussex) (AO 130/11) and aff. to 2nd Home Counties Field Company, Royal Engineers. Redes. **St. Leonards Collegiate School Cadet Company** and transferred to 2nd Home Counties Brigade, RFA by AO 188/14.

76. Colston's School (Bristol) Cadet Corps: Rec. 22.3.15 (Gloucester) (AO 225/15) and aff. to 4th Bn. Gloucestershire Regt. Inc. to four companies by AO 69/19.

77. Congleton Cadet Corps: Rec. 24.2.17 (Chester) (AO 128/17) and aff. to 7th Bn. Cheshire Regt.

78. Coopers' Company's School Cadet Corps: Rec. 10.10.11 (City of London) (AO 11/12) and aff. to 5th Bn. London Regt. Amal. with Parmiters School Cadet Corps to form **2nd City of London Cadet Battalion (Secondary Schools)** by AO 229/16.

79. Cordwallis Cadet Company: Rec. 3.5.18 (Berks) (AO 209/18) and aff. to 1st Bn. Berkshire Volunteer Regt. Transferred to the admin. of Surrey TFA and became part of 2nd Cadet Bn. Royal West Surrey Regt. by AO 24/29.

80. Cornwall, 1st Cadet Battalion of: The battalion was aff. to 4th Bn. Duke of Cornwall's Light Infantry and its companies formed as follows:- "A" rec. 1.11.13 (AO 398/13). Disbanded by AO 323/21. "B" rec. 25.6.15 (AO 302/15). "C" rec. 18.8.15 (AO 343/15). "D" rec. 9.10.15 (AO 430/15). Disbanded by AO 514/20. "E" rec. 19.2.16 (AO 96/16). "F" rec. 17.9.17 (AO 360/17). Disbanded by AO 103/19. "H" Company redesignated as "F" by AO 340/19. Disbanded by AO 323/21. "G" rec. 20.1.18 (AO 149/18). Disbanded by AO 340/19. New "G" rec. 6.8.19 (AO 340/19) aff. to 5th Bn. DCLI and designated **Church Loyalty Guards.** "H" rec. 21.3.18 (AO 149/18) and aff. to 1st Bn. Cornwall Volunteer Regt. Redes. as "F" Company by AO 340/19. Transferred to 4th Bn. DCLI by AO 116/20. **The Isles of Scilly Company** rec. 30.4.18 (AO 173/18) and aff. to 1st Bn. Cornwall Volunteer Regt. Transferred to 4th Bn. DCLI by AO 116/20. Disbanded by AO 452/21. Admin. by Cornwall TFA.

81. Cotham Secondary School Cadet Corps: See Merchant Venturers, Bristol.

82. Coventry Cadet Battalion, 1st, Church Lads Brigade: See 2nd Worcester (Coventry) Cadet Bn. CLB.

83. Coventry Cadet Battalion, 2nd, Church Lads Brigade: See 3rd Birmingham Cadet Bn. CLB.

84. Coventry Cadet Company, 2nd, The Boys Brigade: Rec. 27.6.19 (Warwick) (AO 276/19).

85. Coventry Company, Catholic Cadets: Rec. 1.6.18 (Warwick) (AO 240/18). Inc. to three companies by AO 317/20.

86. Coventry Ordnance Works Cadet Corps: Rec. 23.9.18 (Warwick) (AO 103/19).

87. Cowley Cadet Corps: Rec. 25.6.10 (Oxford) (AO 197/10) and aff. to 4th Bn. Oxfordshire and Buckinghamshire Light Infantry.

88. Cranbrook College (Ilford) Cadets: Rec. 22.4.14 (Essex) (AO 188/14) and aff. to 4th Bn. Essex Regt. Redes. **3rd Cadet Bn. Essex Regt.** by AO 96/16.

89. Cranleigh Cadet Corps, Church Lads Brigade: See Winchester Cadet Bn. CLB.

90. Crediton Grammar School Cadet Corps: Rec. 3.8.15 (Devon) (AO 343/15) and aff. to 6th Bn. Devonshire Regt. Inc. to two companies by AO 111/18.

91. Crewe Cadet Corps: Rec. 22.11.17 (Chester) (AO 51/18) and aff. to 4th Bn. Cheshire Volunteer Regt. Rec. withdrawn by AO 61/20.

92. Crewkerne School Cadet Company: Rec. 14.3.18 (Somerset) (AO 149/18) and aff. to 3rd Bn. Somerset Volunteer Regt. Transfered to 5th Bn. Somerset Light Infantry by AO 116/20.

93. Criccieth Cadet Company: Rec. 17.3.21 (Carnarvon) (AO 184/21) and aff. to 6th Bn. Royal Welsh Fusiliers.

94. Cripplegate Cadet Company: Rec. 1.5.19 (City of London) (AO 251/19) and aff. to 1st Bn. London Regt. Disbanded by AO 61/20.

95. Croydon High School Cadet Corps: Rec. 2.10.16 (Surrey) (AO 375/16) and aff. to 4th Bn. Royal West Surrey Regt. Absorbed into 1st Cadet Bn. Royal West Surrey Regt. by AO 103/19.

96. Crypt Grammar School Cadet Corps: Rec. 18.6.17 (Gloucester) (AO 275/17) and aff. to 5th Bn. Gloucestershire Regt. Inc. to two companies by AO 401/22.

97. Cwn Cadet Company: See 3rd Cadet Bn. Monmouthshire Regt.

D

1. Dartmouth Cadet Company: Rec. 14.12.10 (Devon) (AO 11/11) and aff. to 7th Bn. Devonshire Regt. Transferred to 5th Bn. by AO 514/20.

2. De Aston School (Market Rasen) Cadet Company: Rec. 8.3.16 (Lincoln) (AO 160/19) and aff. to 4th Bn. Lincolnshire Regt.

3. Denbigh County School Cadet Corps: Rec. 23.11.16 (Denbigh) (AO 24/17) and aff. to 4th Bn. Royal Welsh Fusiliers. Disbanded by AO 323/21.

4. Depot, Royal Marine Cadet Corps: Rec. 2.6.13 (Kent) (AO 274/13) and aff. to 4th Bn. East Kent Regt.

5. Derby Cadet Battalion, 1st, The Boys Brigade: Rec. 30.7.17 (Derby) (AO 360/17).

6. Derby Municipal Secondary School Cadet Corps: Rec. 7.8.16 (Derby) (AO 302/16). Aff. to 5th Bn. Notts and Derby Regt. by AO 335/16. Absorbed into Derbyshire Schools Cadet Bn. by AO 219/19.

7. Derby Post Office Cadet Corps: Rec. 6.6.10 (Derby) (AO 197/10) and aff. to 5th Bn. Notts and Derby Regt. Rec. withdrawn 6.12.13 (AO 10/14).

8. Derbyshire Schools Cadet Battalion: Rec. 1.2.19 (Derby) (AO 219/19) and formed by the amal. of- Mount St. Mary's College, Buxton College, Chesterfield Grammar School, Derby Municipal Secondary School, Ilkeston County School, Wirksworth Grammar School, Queen Elizabeth's Ashbourne and Tideswell Grammar School cadet units. Battalion aff. to Notts and Derby Regt. Reduced to seven companies by AO 317/20. Reduced to five companies by AO 25/21.

9. Devon (Fortress) Royal Engineers: No 1 Cadet Company see Yealmpton Cadet Corps. **No 2 Cadet Company** rec. 2.1.12 (AO 41/12). Redes. **No 2 (Plymouth) Cadet Company** by AO 290/12. Absorbed 1st Cadet Company, 2nd Volunteer Bn. Devonshire Regt. by AO 514/20. All units admin. by Devon TFA.

10. Devonport High School Cadet Corps: Rec. 17.3.15 (Devon) (AO 225/15) and aff. to 5th Bn. Devonshire Regt.

11. Devonshire Regt., 1st Cadet Company, 1st Volunteer Battalion: Rec. 25.9.18 (Devon) (AO 342/18). Aff. to 5th Bn. Devonshire Regt. by AO 116/20. Absorbed into No 2 (Plymouth) Cadet Company, Devon (Fortress) Royal Engineers by AO 514/20.

12. Dewsbury Company Cadets, 1st, The Boys Brigade: Rec. 27.7.18 (West Yorks) (AO 307/18).

13. Dolgelly County School Cadets: See 1st Cadet Company, 7th Bn. Royal Welsh Fusiliers.

14. Doncaster Grammar School Cadet Corps: Rec. 24.1.15 (West Yorks) (AO 139/15) and aff. to 5th Bn. Yorkshire Light Infantry.

15. Dorchester Cadet Company, 2nd, The Boys Brigade: Rec. 21.1.18 (Dorset) (AO 149/18).

16. Dorking High School Cadet Corps: Rec. 15.11.15 (Surrey) (AO 457/15) and aff. to 5th Bn. Royal West Surrey Regt. Became part of 2nd Cadet Bn. Royal West Surrey Regt. by AO 103/19.

17. Douai School (Woolhampton) Cadet Company: Rec. 13.11.15 (Berks) (AO 457/15) and aff. to 4th Bn. Royal Berkshire Regt. Disbanded by AO 265/22.

18. Drax Grammar School Cadet Company: Rec. 3.3.14 (West Yorks) (AO 104/14).

19. Dudley Boys Brigade Cadet Company: Rec. 18.9.20 (Worcester) (AO 514/20) and aff. to 7th Bn. Worcestershire Regt.

20. Dudley Cadet Corps: Rec. 24.5.18 (Worcester) (AO 209/18) and aff. to 1st Volunteer Bn. Worcestershire Regt. Transfered to 7th Bn. by AO 116/29. Disbanded by AO 493/21.

21. Dudley Grammar School Cadet Company: See 2nd Cadet Bn. Worcestershire Regt.

22. Dumfries Academy Cadet Corps: Rec. 8.3.17 (Dumfries) (AO 128/17) and aff. to 5th Bn. King's Own Scottish Borderers.

23. Dundee Companies, The Boys Brigade: 1st rec. 20.7.20 (AO 371/20). **2nd** rec. 19.2.19 (AO 137/19). **3rd (YMCA)** rec. 19.2.19 (AO 137/19). **4th** rec. 19.2.19 (AO 137/19). Disbanded by AO 452/21. **6th** rec. 1.10.20 (AO 514/20). **8th** rec. 19.2.19 (AO 137/19). **9th** rec. 19.4.21 (AO 271/21). **10th** rec. 19.2.19 (AO 137/19). **14th** rec. 19.2.19 (AO 137/19). **15th** rec. 31.8.20 (AO 406/20). **16th** rec. 1.10.20 (AO 514/20). **19th** rec. 16.5.22 (AO 265/22). **20th** rec. 19.2.19 (AO 137/19). **22nd** rec. 19.2.19 (AO 137/19). **23rd** rec. 21.11.22 (AO 483/22). **24th** rec. 19.2.19 (AO 137/19). **26th** rec. 20.7.20 (AO 371/20). **32nd** rec. 21.10.21 (AO 265/22). **33rd** rec. 21.10.21 (AO 493/21). All units admin. by Dundee TFA.

24. Dunoon Grammar School Cadet Corps: Rec. 19.10.10 (Argyll) (AO 309/10) and aff. to 8th Bn. Argyll and Sutherland Highlanders.

25. Dunstable Grammar School Cadet Corps: Rec. 1.6.14 (Bedford) (AO 103/19) and aff. to 5th Bn. Bedfordshire and Hertfordshire Regt.

26. Durham Company, 1st, Boys Brigade Cadets: Rec. 23.3.18 (Durham) (AO 209/18). Rec. withdrawn by AO 95/22.

27. Durham Company, 2nd, The Boys Brigade: Rec. 25.8.21 (Durham) (AO 493/21).

28. Durham, County of, Cadet Battalion, 1st: Rec. 30.4.11 (Durham) (AO 191/11).

29. Durham, County of, Cadet Battalion, 2nd, Church Lads Brigade: Rec. 30.4.11 (Durham) (AO 375/16). Disbanded by AO 493/21.New unit rec. 24.5.22 (AO 265/22) under title, **2nd Durham Cadet Bn. CLB.**

30. Durham, County of, Cadet Battalion, 3rd, Church Lads Brigade: Rec. 30.4.11 (Durham) (AO 375/16).

31. Durham, County of, Cadet Battalion, 4th, Church Lads Brigade: Rec. 30.4.11 (Durham) (AO 375/16).

32. Durham, County of, Cadet Battalion, 5th, Church Lads Brigade: Rec. 30.4.11 (Durham) (AO 375/16).

33. Durham, County of, Cadet Battalion, 7th, Church Lads Brigade: Rec. 30.4.11 (Durham) (AO 375/16).

E

1. Ealing Cadet Battalion, The Boys Brigade: Rec. 25.10.20 (Middlesex) (AO 555/20) . Inc. to five companies by AO 265/22. Reduced to three companies by AO 29/23.

2. Ealing Cadet Company: Rec. 26.9.10 (Middlesex) (AO 281/10) and aff. to 8th Bn. Middlesex Regt. Became part of 2nd Cadet Bn. Middlesex Regt. by AO 96/16.

3. Ealing County School Cadet Company: Rec. 26.10.14 (Middlesex) (AO 511/14) and aff. to 8th Bn. Middlesex Regt. Became part of 2nd Cadet Bn. Middlesex Regt. by AO 96/16.

4. East Anglian Brigade Royal Field Artillery. 85th, 1st Cadet Battery: Rec. 22.2.21 (Essex) (AO 184/21).

5. Eastbourne Municipal Secondary School Cadet Corps: Rec. 10.4.16 (Sussex) (AO 160/16). Disbanded 15.4.17 (AO 111/18).

6. East Derham Cadet Company, Church Lads Brigade: Rec. 12.7.13 (Norfolk) (AO 274/13).

7. East Ham Cadets: See 17th South Essex Company, Boys Brigade.

8. East Ham Secondary School Cadets: Rec. 18.11.14 (Essex) (AO 511/14) and aff. to 4th Bn. Essex Regt. Became part of 5th (Schools) Cadet Bn. Essex Regt. by AO 335/16.

9. East Isle of Wight Cadet Company: Rec. 24.9.15 (Southampton) (AO 430/15) and aff. to 8th Bn. Hampshire Regt. Absorbed into 3rd Cadet (Isle of Wight) Bn. Hampshire Regt. by AO 457/15.

10. East Kent Regt., 1st Volunteer Battalion Cadet Corps: Rec. 17.4.19 (Kent) (AO 219/19). Aff. to 4th Bn. East Kent Regt. by AO 116/20. Transferred to 59th Home Counties Brigade RFA by AO 401/22.

11. East Lancashire Regt.,1st Cadet Battalion: Rec. 14.4.16 (East Lancs) (AO 229/16) and aff. to 4th Bn. Inc. to five companies by AO 51/18. Reduced to three companies by AO 24/20. Reduced to two companies by AO 95/22.

12. East Lancashire Regt.,2nd Cadet Battalion: Rec. 4.10.18 (East Lancs) (AO 373/18) and aff. to 5th Bn.

13. East Riding Cadet Field Ambulance: See 1st Cadet Field Ambulance.

14. East Surrey Regt.,1st Cadet Battalion: Rec. 21.10.18 (Surrey) (AO 103/19) and formed by the amal. of Richmond County School, Richmond Hill, Wimbledon College, Tiffin School and Kingston Grammar School cadet units. Aff. to 6th Bn. Reduced to four companies by AO 95/22.

15. East Surrey Regt.,2nd Cadet Battalion: Rec. 21.10.18 (Surrey) (AO 103/19) and formed by the amal. of Wimbledon and Richmond Boys Naval Brigades. Transfered to the admin. of the Admiralty by AO 251/19.

16. East Surrey Regt.,2nd (Streatham) Cadet Battalion: See 1st Cadet Bn. 15th County of London Volunteer Regt.

17. East Surrey Regt.,3rd Cadet Company, 6th Battalion: Rec. 19.4.15 (Surrey) (AO 225/15). Redes. **St. George's College Cadets** by AO 262/16. Became part of 2nd Cadet Bn. Royal West Surrey Regt. by AO 103/19.

18. East Yorkshire Cadets, Royal Engineers, No 1: Rec. 14.8.18 (East Yorks) (AO 342/18) and aff. to East Riding Volunteer Engineers.

19. East Yorkshire Volunteer Regt.,1st Battalion Cadet Company: Rec. 26.3.18 (East Yorks) (AO 173/18).

20. East Yorkshire Volunteer Regt.,2nd Battalion Cadet Company: Rec. 26.3.18 (East Yorks) (AO 173/18).

21. Ebbw Vale Territorial Cadet Company: Rec. 7.9.10 (Monmouth) (AO 258/10) and aff. to 3rd Bn. Monmouthshire Regt. Became part of 1st Cadet Bn. Monmouthshire Regt. by AO 233/12.

22. Eccleshill Cadet Company, Church Lads Brigade: Rec. 10.8.11 (Stafford) (AO 75/12). Disbanded by AO 398/13.

23. Edinburgh Boys Brigade: The following companies rec. 8.4.18 (AO 173/18):- **1st, 3rd, 5th** (rec. withdrawn by AO 435/22), **7th, 9th, 12th, 13th, 14th, 15th, 16th, 18th** (rec. withdrawn by AO 435/22), **20th, 21st, 22nd** (rec. withdrawn by AO 435/22), **23rd, 24th, 25th, 26th, 28th, 29th, 30th, 31st** (rec. withdrawn by AO 435/22), **32nd, 33rd, 34th, 35th, 39th, 40th, 41st, 42nd, 43rd, 44th, 46th,** (rec. withdrawn by AO 435/22), **47th, 48th, 50th, 51st 52nd, 53rd, 54th, 55th and 56th. 2nd** rec 22.7.20 (AO 371/20). Rec. withdrawn by AO 435/22. **4th** rec. 7.4.21 (AO 271/21). **6th** rec. 7.4.21 (AO 271/21). **10th** rec. 30.11.21 (AO 265/22). **11th** rec. 22.7.20 (AO 371/20). Rec. withdrawn by AO 435/22. **17th** rec. 13.3.22 (AO 265/22). **27th** rec. 30.11.21 (AO 265/22). **36th** rec. 11.1.22 (AO 265/22). **38th** rec. 22.7.20 (AO 371/20). **45th** rec. 30.11.21 (AO 265/22). **58th** rec. 7.1.22 (AO 265/22). All units admin. by City of Edinburgh TFA.

24. Edinburgh, City of, Volunteer Regt., 1st Cadet Battalion: Rec. 29.11.17 (City of Edinburgh) (AO 51/18). Redes. **1st (Edinburgh) Cadet Battalion, Royal Scots** by AO 373/18. Redes. **1st Territorial Cadet Battalion, Royal Scots** by AO 419/19. Aff. to 4th Bn. by AO 116/20.

25. Egremont (St. John's with Columbus) Cadet Company, 1st: Rec. 21.2.13 (Chester) (AO 121/13) and aff. to 4th Bn. Cheshire Regt. Became part of the Church Lads Brigade and aff. to 4th Bn. Cheshire Regt. cancelled by AO 257/14. Disbanded by AO 493/21.

26. Elmfield College (York) Cadet Corps: Rec. 26.10.16 (North Yorks) (AO 406/16) and aff. to 5th Bn. Yorkshire Regt. Became part of the Cadet Battalion, 5th Yorkshire Regt. by AO 116/20.

27. Ely Regiment, 1st Battalion, Church Lads Brigade: Rec. 31.5.11 (Bedford) (AO 191/11). Redes. **3rd St. Albans Cadet Bn. CLB** by AO 104/14.

28. Enfield Cadet Battalion, The Boys Brigade: Rec. 15.7.18 (Middlesex) (AO 307/18). Inc. to seven companies by AO 555/20. Inc. to eight companies by AO 226/21.

29. Enfield Grammar School Cadet Corps: Rec. 29.3.15 (Middlesex) (AO 255/15) and aff. to 7th Bn. Middlesex Regt. Became part of 1st Cadet Bn. Middlesex Regt. by AO 96/16.

30. Engineers Cadets, Royal (2nd London Division): See Kensington Cadet Corps.

31. Epworth College (Rhyl) Cadet Corps: Rec. 16.2.17 (Flint) (AO 95/17). Became part of 1st Cadet Bn. 5th Bn. Royal Welsh Fusiliers by AO 240/18.

32. Essex Cadet Battalion. 1st, The Boys Brigade: Rec. 25.2.18 (Essex) (AO 173/18). Absorbed 2nd Bn. 4.2.19 (AO 137/19.

33. Essex Cadet Battalion, 2nd, The Boys Brigade: Rec. 25.2.18 (Essex) (AO 173/18). Absorbed into 1st Bn. 4.2.19 (AO 137/19).

34. Essex Regt., 1st Cadet Battalion: Formed by AO 65/11 and the amal. of the West Ham Cadets, St. Gabriel's Canning Town, St. Matthew's (Custom House) and the Church of the Ascension cadet units. Inc. to four companies by AO 137/19. Reduced to three companies by AO 150/22. Admin. by Essex TFA.

35. Essex Regt.,2nd Cadet Battalion: See Manor Park Cadet Company.

36. Essex Regt.,3rd Cadet Battalion: See Cranbrook College, Ilford.

37. Essex Regt.,4th Cadet Battalion: Rec. 28.4.16 (Essex) (AO 188/16) and aff. to 4th Bn. Reduced to two companies by AO 150/22.

38. Essex Regt.,5th (Schools) Cadet Battalion: Rec. 18.11.14 (Essex) (AO 335/16) and formed by the amal. of East Ham Secondary School, Woodford Loughton School and Leytonstone and Leyton County High School cadet units. Loughton School withdrawn by AO 406/16. Ilford County High School and Bancroft's School Companies added by AO 128/17. Reduced to five companies by AO 184/21. This Army Order also establishes Bancroft's School as an independent unit. Reduced to two companies by AO 150/22.

39. Essex Regt.,6th Cadet Battalion: See Given Wilson Institute.

40. Essex Regt.,7th Cadet Battalion: See Southend Technical School.

41. Essex Regt.,8th Cadet Battalion: Rec. 14.11.17 (Essex) (AO 51/18) and formed by the amal. of Broomfield, Gt. Baddow, Braintree and Bocking, Writtle and Felstead cadet units. Aff. to 5th Bn. Absorbed Wickford Cadets by AO 209/18. Disbanded by AO 514/20.

42. Essex Regt., 9th Cadet Battalion: Formed by AO 111/18 and the amal. of Highfield College and Clark's College cadet units. Absorbed Gt. Wakering and District Cadet Corps by AO 342/18. Admin. by Essex TFA.

43. Essex Regt.,10th Cadet Battalion: Rec. 15.5.18 (Essex) (AO 240/18) and aff. to 7th Bn. Rec. withdrawn by AO 342/18.

44. Essex Regt.,10th Cadet Battalion (Palmer's School): See Palmer's School.

45. Essex Regt.,11th Cadet Battalion: Rec. 18.7.18 (Essex) (AO 307/18) and aff. to 6th Volunteer Bn. Transferred to 5th Bn. by AO 116/20. Reduced to one company by AO 150/22.

46. Essex Regt.,12th Cadet Battalion: See Sir Anthony Browne's School.

47. Essex Royal Engineers, 1st Cadet Company: Rec. 27.6.17 (Essex) (AO 275/17).

48. Eversham Prince Henry's Grammar School Cadet Corps: Rec. 24.5.18 (Worcester) (AO 209/18) and aff. to 8th Bn. Worcestershire Regt. Absorbed into 1st Cadet Bn. Worcestershire Regt. by A.O. 156/20.

49. Exeter Cadet Battalion: Rec. 27.9.16 (Devon) (AO 375/16) and aff. to 4th Bn. Devonshire Regt. Absorbed Exeter Cathedral School Cadet Company by AO 375/16. Inc. to five companies by AO 360/17.

50. Exeter Cathedral School Cadet Company: Rec. 15.3.11 (Devon) (AO 130/11) and aff. to 4th Bn. Devonshire Regt. Became part of Exeter Cadet Bn. by AO 375/16.

51. Exmouth Cadet Company: Rec. 12.12.17 (Devon) (AO 111/18) and aff. to Devon (Fortress) Royal Engineers. Rec. withdrawn by AO 323/21.

52. Eye Grammar School Cadet Corps: Rec. 1.11.20 (Suffolk) (AO 555/20) and aff. to 5th Bn. Suffolk Regt.

F

1. Fagley YMCA Cadet Unit: Rec. 14.3.22 (West Yorks) (AO 265/22) and aff. to 6th Bn. West Yorks Regt.

2. Fairfield Cadet Corps: Rec. 27.9.18 (City of Glasgow) (AO 373/18) and aff. to 6th Bn. Highland Light Infantry. Inc. to three companies by AO 527/21.

3. Fairfield School (Bristol) Cadet Corps: Rec. 22.3.15 (Gloucester) (AO 225/15) and aff. to 6th Bn. Gloucestershire Regt.

4. Fakenham School Cadet Corps: Rec. 1.4.16 (Norfolk) (AO 160/16) and aff. to 5th Bn. Norfolk Regt. Inc. to three companies by AO 419/19. Disbanded by AO 355/22.

5. Falkirk Company, 3rd, The Boys Brigade Cadets: Rec. 3.5.21 (Stirling) (AO 398/21).

6. Farm School Cadet Battalion: Rec. 13.1.19 (Surrey) (AO 103/19) and aff. to 5th Bn. Royal West Surrey Regt. Reduced to five companies by AO 150/22.

7. Farnham Cadet Corps (The Queen's): See West Surrey Cadets.

8. Farnham Grammar School Cadet Corps: Rec. 10.1.16 (Surrey) (AO 62/16) and aff. to 5th Bn. Royal West Surrey Regt. Became part of 2nd Cadet Bn. Royal West Surrey Regt. by AO 103/19.

9. Felstead School Cadet Company: Rec. 14.10.16 (Essex) (AO 24/17) and aff. to 5th Bn. Essex Regt. Became part of 8th Cadet Bn. Essex Regt. by AO 51/18.

10. Field Artillery, Royal, Fulham Cadets: See Fulham Cadet Corps.

11. Fife and Forfar Armoured Car Cadet Company, 2nd: Rec. 25.11.21 (Fife) (AO 527/21).

12. Fife, County of, Cadet Battalion, 1st: Rec. 19.4.15 (Fife) (AO 261/15) and aff. to 7th Bn. Black Watch. Disbanded by AO 255/20.

13. Finchley Company, 2nd, The Boys Brigade Cadets: Rec. 15.7.18 (Middlesex) (AO 307/18).

14. Finchley Cadet Company, 3rd, The Boys Brigade: Rec. 30.1.22 (Middlesex) (AO 265/22).

15. Finlay Street School Cadets: Rec. 17.2.19 (County of London) (AO 219/19). Disbanded by AO 116/20.

16. Fletton Secondary School Cadet Corps: Rec. 10.3.16 (Hunts) (AO 125/16) and aff. to Hunts Cyclist Bn. Disbanded by AO 493/21.

17. Forest Cadet Corps (Walthamstow): Rec. 28.9.10 (Essex) (AO 281/10) and aff. to 7th Bn. Essex Regt. Rec. withdrawn by AO 320/12.

18. Forest Hill House School Cadets: Rec. 5.5.19 (County of London) (AO 251/19). Disbanded by AO 514/20.

19. Framlingham Cadet Company: Rec. 8.7.18 (Suffolk) (AO 307/18). Disbanded by AO 452/21.

20 **Friars School Cadet Corps:** Rec. 12.12.17 (Carnarvon) (AO 111/18). Disbanded by AO 219/19.

21. **Friern Barnet School Cadet Company:** Rec. 22.12.14 (Middlesex) (AO 79/15) and aff. to 7th Bn. Middlesex Regt. Became part of 1st Cadet Bn. Middlesex Regt. by AO 96/16.

22. **Frimley and Camberley Cadet Corps:** Rec. 15.1.12 (Surrey) (AO 41/12) and aff. to 5th Bn. Royal West Surrey Regt. Disbanded by AO 149/18. Re-rec. by AO 340/19.

23. **Fulham Cadet Corps:** Rec. 16.5.19 (County of London) (AO 251/19) and aff. to 20th Bn. County of London Volunteer Regt. Transfered to 7th London Brigade RFA by AO 116/20. Redes. **Royal Field Artillery (Fulham) Cadets** by AO 493/21.

24. **Fusiliers, Royal, 1st Cadet Battalion:** Rec. 1.1.11 (City of London) (AO 65/11). Reduced to eight companies by AO 198/22. Reduced to four companies by AO 483/22. See also Lord Robert's Boys, Broomsleigh Street School and 7th Bn. London Regt. cadet units.

25. **Fusiliers, Royal, 2nd Cadet Battalion (Secondary Schools):** Formed by (AO 72/21) and the amal. of Haberdashers and Northern Polytechnic Schools cadet units. Reduced to seven companies by AO 493/21. Admin. by City of London TFA.

G

1. **Gainsborough Cadet Company, The Boys Brigade:** Rec. 17.7.17 (Lincoln) (AO 360/17).

2. **Galashiels Companies, 1st and 2nd, The Boys Brigade:** Rec. 12.2.19 (Selkirk) (AO 137/19).

3. **George Green's School (Poplar) Cadet Corps:** Rec. 25.2.16 (City of London) (AO 125/16). Aff. to 17th Bn. London Regt. by AO 262/16.Amal. with Raines School, Stepney to form **3rd City of London Cadet Battalion:** by AO 275/17.

4. **Given Wilson Institute Cadets:** Rec. 23.12.14 (Essex) (AO 41/15) and aff. to 6th Bn. Essex Regt. Redes. **6th Cadet Bn. Essex Regt.** by AO 168/17. Reduced to one company by AO 401/22.

5. **Glasgow, City of, Cadet Battalion, 1st:** Rec. 11.5.15 (City of Glasgow) (AO 302/15). Aff. to 5th Bn. Highland Light Infantry by AO 360/17. Reduced to one company by AO 527/21.

6. **Glasgow, City of, Cadet Battalion, 2nd:** Rec. 11.5.15 (City of Glasgow) (AO 302/15). Aff. to 7th Bn. Cameronians by AO 406/16.Reduced to two companies by AO 527/21.

7. **Glasgow, City of, Cadet Battalion, 3rd:** Rec. 11.5.15 (City of Glasgow) (AO 302/15). Aff. to 5th Bn. Cameronians by AO 111/18. Redes. **5th The Cameronians (Scottish Rifles) Cadet Battalion** by AO 514/20. Reduced to four companies by AO 527/21.

8. Glasgow Companies, The Boys Brigade: The following companies rec. 1.12.17 (AO 111/18), 4th, 5th, 6th, 8th, 9th, 10th, 11th. 15th, 17th. 31st, 32nd, 35th, 37th, 42nd, 45th, 50th (disbanded by AO 527/21), 52nd, 55th, 60th, 62nd, 73rd, 76th, 79th, 81st, 86th (disbanded by AO 116/20), 88th, 90th, 91st, 92nd, 95th, 99th (disbanded by AO 116/20), 100th, 102nd, 104th, 106th, 107th 110th, 112th, 113th, 115th, 116th, 118th, 122nd, 127th, 137th. 139th, 140th, 141st, 143rd, 145th, 146th, 154th, 160th, 163rd, 164th and 167th. The following companies rec. 1.7.21 (AO 452/21) 34th, 80th, 84th, 86th, 89th, 105th, 156th, 184th, (rec. withdrawn by AO 435/22) and 198th. Other companies recognised were, 18th (19.6.18 AO 240/18), 19th (5.3.18 AO 149/18), 41st (5.3.18 AO 149/18), 51st (5.3.18 AO 149/18), 57th (6.9.18 AO 342/18), 64th (21.6.18 AO 240/18), 65th (19.6.18 AO 240/18), 82nd (27.9.18 AO 342/18), 85th (5.3.18 AO 149/18), 98th (18.5.22 AO 265/22), 108th (27.1.19 AO 102/19), 136th (24.4.18 AO 173/18), 144th (29.9.21 AO 527/21), 147th (6.9.18 AO 342/18) disbanded by AO 527/21, 149th (28.11.21 AO 265/22), 159th (12.11.18 AO 31/19), 173rd (18.5.22 AO 265/22), 200th (28.11.21 AO 265/22). All units admin. by City of Glasgow TFA.

9. Glasgow Company, Jewish Lads Brigade: Rec. 11.5.15 (City of Glasgow) (AO 430/15). Inc. to two companies by AO 406/20. Reduced to one company by AO 527/21.

10. Glasgow Postal Telegraph Messengers Cadet Corps: Rec. 29.6.10 (City of Glasgow) (AO 281/10) and aff. to 9th Bn. Highland Light Infantry.

11. Gloucester Battalion, 1st, Church Lads Brigade: Rec. 18.9.11 (Gloucester) (AO 316/11). Reduced to four companies by AO 355/22.

12. Gloucester Battalion, 2nd, Church Lads Brigade: Rec. 18.12.11 (Gloucester) (AO 41/12). Redes. **1st Bristol Cadet Bn.** CLB and inc. to thirteen companies by AO 251/19. Reduced to six companies by AO 401/22.

13. Gloucestershire Regt.,6th Bn.,1st and 2nd Cadet Companies: Rec. 18.12.12 (Gloucester) (AO 49/13).

14. Gordon Boys Home Cadet Corps: Rec. 11.3.12 (Surrey) (AO 109/12). Inc. to four companies by AO 116/20.

15. Gordon Highlanders,6th Bn.,"A" Cadet Company: Rec. 29.3.18 (County of Aberdeen) (AO 209/18). Rec. withdrawn by AO 29/23.

16. Gourock Cadet Companies, 1st, 2nd and 3rd, The Boys Brigade: Rec. 14.2.18 (Renfrew) (AO 149/18).

17. Great Baddow Cadet Company: Rec. 28.4.16 (Essex) (AO 188/16) and aff. to 5th Bn. Essex Regt. Became part of 8th Cadet Bn. Essex Regt. by AO 51/18.

18. Great Wakering and District Cadet Corps: Rec. 26.1.16 (Essex) (AO 125/16) and aff. to 6th Bn. Essex Regt. Became part of 9th Cadet Bn. Essex Regt. by AO 342/18.

19. Great Yarmouth Grammar School Cadets: Rec. 29.5.15 (Norfolk) (AO 261/15) and aff. to 1st East Anglian Brigade RFA. Transfered to 4th Bn. Norfolk Regt. by AO 365/21.

20. Green Park College Cadet Company: Rec. 4.5.18 (Somerset) (AO 209/18) and aff. to 2nd Volunteer Bn. Somerset Light Infantry. Disbanded by AO 219/19.

21. Greenwich Naval Cadet Unit: Rec. 19.1.12 (County of London) (AO 143/12). Disbanded by AO 219/19.

22. Grimsby and Cleethorpes Company: see 3rd Lincoln Cadet Bn.

23. Grove Academy Cadet Company: Rec. 18.6.18 (City of Dundee) (AO 307/18) and aff. to City of Dundee Volunteer Regt. Transfered to 4th Bn. Black Watch by AO 116/20.

24. Grove Park School (Wrexham) Cadet Unit: Rec. 28.10.15 (Denbigh) (AO 457/15) and aff. to 4th Bn. Royal Welsh Fusiliers.

25. Guild Street Cadet Corps: Rec. 18.6.18 (Stafford) (AO 240/18) and aff. to 2nd Bn. Staffordshire Volunteer Regt. Disbanded by AO 95/22.

26. Guisborough Grammar School Cadet Corps: Rec. 29.4.15 (North Yorks) (AO 225/15) and aff. to 4th Bn. Yorkshire Regt. Became part of the Cadet Bn. 4th Yorkshire Regt. by AO 116/20.

H

1. Haberdashers (Hampstead) School Cadet Corps: Rec. 9.12.14 (City of London) (AO 79/15). Transferred to the admin. of County of London TFA by AO 255/20. Amal. with Northern Polytechnic School to form **2nd Cadet Bn. Royal Fusiliers** by AO 72/21.

2. Haddington Cadet Corps: Rec. 6.6.10 (Haddington) (AO 258/10) and aff. to 8th Bn. Royal Scots. Transferred to 57th (Lowland) Medium Brigade RGA by AO 72/21.

3. Halesowen Grammar School Cadet Company: Rec. 26.6.15 (Worcester) (AO 302/15) and aff. to 7th Bn. Worcestershire Regt. Became part of Worcestershire Cadet Bn. by AO 188/16.

4. Haltwhistle Territorial Cadets: Rec. 24.11.10 (Northumberland) (AO 11/11) and aff. to 4th Bn. Northumberland Fusiliers. Rec. withdrawn by AO 229/16.

5. Hamilton Cadet Company, 1st, The Boys Brigade: Rec. 15.11.21 (Lanark) (AO 265/22).

6. Hamilton Cadet Company, 2nd, The Boys Brigade: Rec. 20.12.21 (Lanark) (AO 265/22).

7. Hampshire, 1st Cadet Battalion of: Rec. 15.12.11 (Southampton) (AO 109/12). Redes. **1st Cadet Battalion, Hampshire Regt.** and aff. to 6th Bn. by AO 337/13. Amal. with Peter Symonds School and Aldershot County School to form **1/4th and 2/4th Hampshire Regt. Cadet Battalions** by AO 307/18. 2/4th inc. to nine companies by AO 219/19. 1/4th reduced to six companies by AO 211/10. "E" Company of 1/4th redes. **Farnham Cadet Corps (The Queen's),** transferred to the admin. of Surrey TFA and aff. to 5th Bn. Royal West Surrey Regt. by AO 25/21. See also West Surrey Cadets.

8. Hampshire Regt., 1st Cadet Battalion: See 1st Cadet Bn. of Hampshire.

9. Hampshire Regt., 2nd Cadet Battalion: Rec. 10.9.14 (Southampton) (AO 451/14) and aff. to 6th Bn. Redes. **6th Hampshire Regt. Cadet Bn.** by AO 307/18. Inc. to thirteen companies by AO 24/20. Reduced to two companies by AO 435/22.

10. **Hampshire Regt,3rd Cadet (Isle of Wight) Battalion:** Rec. 28.4.11 (Southampton) (AO 457/15) and formed by the amal. of Ventnor, Ryde, Shanklin, East Isle of Wight, Cowes, Sandown and Newport Cadet Companies. Aff. to 8th Bn. Redes. **8th Hampshire Regt. (Isle of Wight) Cadet Bn.** by AO 307/18. Reduced to six companies by AO 156/20. Reduced to five companies by AO 211/20.Reduced to four companies by AO 555/20. "B" Company redes. **1st (Ryde) Cadet Company** by AO 25/21.

11. **Hampshire Regt. 1/4th and 2/4th Cadet Battalions:** See 1st Cadet Bn. of Hampshire.

12. **Hampshire Regt.,5th Cadet Battalion:** Formed by AO 307/18 and the amal. of King Edward VI School, Southampton and Tauntons School cadet units. Amal. with 7th Hampshire Regt. Cadet Bn. to form **5/7th Hampshire Regt. Cadet Bn.** by AO 150/22. Reduced to eight companies by AO 435/22. Admin. by Southampton TFA.

13. **Hampshire Regt.,5/7th Cadet Battalion:** See 5th Cadet Bn.

14. **Hampshire Regt.,6th Cadet Battalion:** See 2nd Cadet Bn.

15. **Hampshire Regt.,7th Cadet Battalion:**Rec. 29.11.17 (Southampton) (AO 307/18). Amal. with 5th Hampshire Regt. Cadet Bn. by AO 150/22.

16. **Hampshire Regt.,8th (Isle of Wight) Cadet Battalion:** See 3rd Cadet (Isle of Wight) Cadet Bn..

17. **Harborne Training School Cadet Corps:** Rec. 26.1.17 (Warwick) (AO 95/17) and aff. to 6th Bn. Royal Warwickshire Regt.

18. **Harringay Cadet Company:** Rec. 22.12.14 (Middlesex) (AO 79/15) and aff. to 7th Bn. Middlesex Regt. Became part of 1st Cadet Bn. Middlesex Regt. by AO 96/16.

19. **Harrogate Company Catholic Boys Brigade:** Rec. 5.1.14 (West Yorks) (AO 38/14).

20. **Harrow Cadet Company:** Rec. 12.12.10 (Middlesex) (AO 40/11) and aff. to 9th Bn. Middlesex Regt. Became part of 3rd Cadet Bn. Middlesex Regt. by AO 96/16.

21.**Hartlebury Grammar School Cadet Corps:** Rec.26.1.18 (Worcester) (AO 149/18) and aff. to 7th Bn. Worcestershire Regt. Absorbed into 1st Cadet Bn. Worcestershire Regt. by AO 156/20.

22. **Hartlepool Company, 1st, The Boys Brigade:** Rec. 18.6.19 (Durham) (AO 276/19).

23. **Hartlepool Company. The Catholic Cadets:** Rec. 14.7.22 (Durham) (AO 310/22).

24. **Hastings Cadet Company, 1st, The Boys Brigade:** Rec. 3.8.22 (Sussex) (AO 483/22).

25. **Haverstock Central School Cadet Corps:** Rec. 30.11.15 (City of London) (AO 96/16). Disbanded by AO 118/21.

26. **Hawarden County School Cadet Corps:** Rec. 22.6.16 (Flint) (AO 302/16) and aff. to 5th Bn. Royal Welsh Fusiliers. Became part of 1st Cadet Bn. Royal Welsh Fusiliers by AO 240/18.

27. Haytor (Newton Abbot) Cadet Corps: Rec. 2.1.12 (Devon) (AO 75/12) and aff. to 5th Bn. Devonshire Regt. Redes. **Newton Abbot Cadet Corps** by AO 375/16.

28. Helensburgh Company, 1st, The Boys Brigade Cadets: Rec. 5.9.17 (Dumbarton) (AO 360/17).

29. Henley Royal Grammar School Cadet Corps: Rec. 18.6.20 (Oxford) (AO 459/20) and aff. to 4th Bn. Oxfordshire and Buckinghamshire Light Infantry.

30. Hereford Cadet Battalion, 1st, Church Lads Brigade: Rec. 10.8.12 (Hereford) (AO 156/13). Redes. **Ludlow Cadet Company CLB.** by AO 493/21.

31. Herefordshire Regt.,1st Cadet Battalion: Rec. 30.4.18 (Hereford) (AO 209/18) and aff. to 1st Volunteer Bn. Herefordshire Regt. Transfered to 1st Bn. Herefordshire Regt. by AO 116/20.

32. Hermitage School (Helensburgh) Cadet Corps: Rec. 15.5.17 (Dumbarton) (AO 275/17) and aff. to 9th Bn. Argyll and Sutherland Highlanders.

33. Hern Bay College Cadet Corps: Rec. 9.1.13 (Kent) (AO 49/13) and aff. to 4th Bn. East Kent Regt. Amal. with New College (Hern Bay) Cadet Corps by AO 95/17.

34. Hertfordshire Cadet Company, 1st (Chorley Wood): Rec. 10.4.11 (Hertford) (AO 161/11) and aff. to 1st Bn. Hertfordshire Regt. Rec. withdrawn 19.12.13 (AO 10/14).

35. Hertfordshire Cadet Company, 2nd (Watford Scouts): Rec. 10.4.11 (Hertford) (AO 161/11) and aff. to 2nd Hertfordshire Battery, RFA. Transfered to 1st Bn. Hertfordshire Regt. by AO 373/13. Disbanded by AO 527/21.

36. Hertfordshire Cadets, 3rd (Stortford School): Rec. 30.10.11 (Hertford) (AO 347/11) and aff. to 1st Bn. Hertfordshire Regt.

37. Hertfordshire Cadets, 4th (St. George's School): Rec. 15.10.13 (Hertford) (AO 398/13) and aff. to 1st Bn. Hertfordshire Regt.

38. Hertfordshire Cadets, 5th (Stortford College): Rec. 23.10.14 (Hertford) (AO 451/14) as **Bishop's Stortford College Cadet Corps** and aff. to 1st Bn. Hertfordshire Regt. Reds. by AO 302/16. Disbanded by AO 527/21.

39. Hertfordshire Cadets, 6th (Watford Grammar School): Rec. 20.2.15 (Hertford) (AO 225/15) and aff. to 1st Bn. Hertfordshire Regt. Inc. to two companies by AO 240/18.

40. Hertfordshire Cadets, 7th (Queen Elizabeth's School Barnet): Rec. 20.2.15 (Hertford) (AO 225/15) and aff. to 1st Bn. Hertfordshire Regt.

41. Hertfordshire Cadets, 8th (St. Edmund's College): Rec. 29.9.16 (Hertford) (AO 375/16) and aff. to 1st Bn. Hertfordshire Regt. Reduced to one company by AO 95/22.

42. Hertfordshire Cadets, 9th: Rec. 28.9.17 (Hertford) (AO 51/18) and aff. to 1st Bn. Hertfordshire Volunteer Regt. Transferred to 1st Bn. Hertfordshire Regt. by AO 116/20. Reduced to one company by AO 95/22.

43. Hertfordshire Cadets. 10th: See Boys Brigade Cadets.

44. Hertfordshire Cadets, 11th: See Royal Masonic School.

45. Hertfordshire Cadets, 12th: Rec. 17.12.17 (Hertford) (AO 149/18) and aff. to 3rd Bn. Hertfordshire Volunteer Regt. Transferred to 1st Bn. Hertfordshire Regt. by AO 116/20. Disbanded by AO 527/21. See also Waltham Abbey Cadet Corps.

46. Hertfordshire Cadets, 13th: Rec. 17.12.17 (Hertford) (AO 149/18) and aff. to 3rd Bn. Hertfordshire Volunteer Regt. Inc. to two companies by AO 240/18. Transferred to 1st Bn. Hertfordshire Regt. by AO 116/20. Reduced to one company by AO 95/22.

47. Hertfordshire Cadets, 14th: Rec. 30.9.18 (Hertford) (AO 342/18) and aff. to 2nd Volunteer Bn. Hertfordshire Regt. Transferred to 1st Bn. Hertfordshire Regt. by AO 116/20. Disbanded by AO 527/21.

48. Hertfordshire Cadets, 15th (St. Michael's School): Rec. 1.11.20 (Hertford) (AO 25/21) and aff. to 1st Bn. Hertfordshire Regt.

49. Heversham Grammar School Cadet Company: Rec. 28.10.15 (Westmoreland) (AO 457/15) and aff. to 4th Bn. Border Regt.

50. Highbury Park School Cadet Corps: Rec. 25.5.21 (County of London) (AO 271/21).

51. Higher Grade School (Colwyn Bay) Cadet Corps: Rec. 20.12.16 (Denbigh) (AO 275/17) and aff. to 4th Bn. Royal Welsh Fusiliers. Disbanded by AO 323/21.

52. Highfield College (Leigh-on-Sea) Cadets: Rec. 29.3.16 (Essex) (AO 160/16) and aff. to 6th Bn. Essex Regt. Amal. with Clark's College Cadets to form **9th Cadet Bn. Essex Regt.** by AO 111/18.

53. Highfield School Cadet Corps: Rec. 15.7.18 (Surrey) (AO 307/18) and aff. to 6th Bn. East Surrey Regt. Redes. **Weybridge Park College Cadet Corps** by AO 340/19. Inc. to two companies by AO 419/19. Reduced to one Company by AO 150/22.

54. High School Cadet Company: Rec. 19.2.18 (City of Dundee) (AO 307/18) and aff. to 2nd Volunteer Bn. Black Watch. Transferred to 4th Bn. by AO 116/20.

55. Histon and Impington Company, 1st, The Boys Brigade Cadets: Rec. 6.10.17 (Cambs and Ely) (AO 360/17). Rec. withdrawn by AO 435/22.

56. Holy Trinity, Aberystwyth Cadet Company, Church Lads Brigade: Rec. 19.4.16 (Carmarthen) (AO 160/16). Absorbed into 2nd St. David's Cadet Bn. CLB by AO 493/21.

57. Holy Trinity, Colne Cadet Company, Church Lads Brigade: Rec. 22.3.16 (West Lancs) (AO 160/16). Rec. withdrawn by AO 51/18.

58. Holy Trinity, Felin Foel, Llanelly Cadet Company, Church Lads Brigade: Rec. 19.4.16 (Carmarthen) (AO 160/16).

59. Holy Trinity, Wilnecote Cadet Company, Church Lads Brigade: Rec. 28.8.17 (Warwick) (AO 360/17). Amal. with 3rd Birmingham Cadet Bn. CLB by AO 31/19. Amal. cancelled by AO 527/21.

60. Home Counties Brigade Royal Field Artillery, 1st, 1st Cadet Battalion: See Imperial Service Cadet Corps, Brighton.

61. Home Counties Divisional Royal Engineers, 44th, Nos 2 and 4 Companies: Rec. 10.10.21 (Sussex) (AO 527/21).

62. Honourable Artillery Company, 1st Cadet Battalion: Rec. 27.12.16 (City of London) (AO 65/17).

63. Horbury Company Cadets, 1st, The Boys Brigade: Rec. 27.7.18 (West Yorks) (AO 307/18).

64. Horbury Company Cadets, 3rd, The Boys Brigade: Rec. 27.7.18 (West Yorks) (AO 307/18).

65. Hove High School Cadet Corps: Rec. 2.4.18 (Sussex) (AO 173/18) and aff. to 4th Bn. Royal Sussex Regt. Disbanded by AO 72/21.

66. Hugh Myddleton School Cadet Corps: Rec. 30.8.11 (City of London) (AO 11/12). Reduced to one company by AO 265/22.

67. Hull Cadet Company, St. Mark's Church Scouts: Rec. 21.5.13 (East Yorks) (AO 235/13). Disbanded by AO 95/17.

68. Hull Grammar School Cadet Corps: Rec. 13.11.16 (East Yorks) (AO 406/16). Aff. to 4th Bn. East Yorkshire Regt. by AO 255/20. Redes. **Hull Grammar School Cadet Bn.** and inc. to four companies by AO 118/21.

69. Hull Orderly Boys: Rec. 22.1.18 (East Yorks) (AO 173/18). Aff. to 4th Bn. East Yorkshire Regt. by AO 255/20.

70. Hulme Grammar School Cadet Corps: Rec. 8.10.15 (East Lancs) (AO 430/15) and aff. to 6th Bn. Manchester Regt. Inc. to two companies by AO 251/19. Reduced to one company by AO 452/21.

71. Huntingdon Grammar School Cadet Corps: Rec. 10.3.16 (Hunts) (AO 125/16). Disbanded by AO 310/22.

72. Hutcheson's Grammar School Cadet Corps: Rec. 8.12.13 (City of Glasgow) (AO 10/14) and aff. to 7th Bn. Cameronians. Reduced to one company by AO 527/21.

73. Hutton Grammar School Cadet Corps: Rec. 19.8.18 (West Lancs) (AO 307/18) and aff. tto 4th Bn. Loyal North Lancs. Regt.

74. Hykeham Company: See 4th Lincoln Cadet Bn.

I

1. Ilford Church Cadets: Rec. 25.1.11 (Essex) (AO 161/11). Inc. to four companies by AO 111/18.

2. Ilford College Cadet Corps: Rec. 29.3.16 (Essex) (AO 160/16) and aff. to 4th Bn. Essex Regt. Rec. withdrawn by AO 251/19.

3. Ilford County High School Cadet Company: Formed by AO 128/17 and added to 5th (Schools) Cadet Bn. Essex Regt. Admin. by Essex TFA.

4. Ilkeston County School Cadet Corps: Rec. 22.1.17 (Derby) (AO 65/17). Absorbed into the Derbyshire Schools Cadet Bn. by AO 219/19.

5. Imperial Cadet Corps, 2nd **(Fulham) Battalion:** Rec. 31.3.11 (City of London) (AO 161/11). Divided by AO 177/12 to form **Ackmar School (LCC) Cadet Corps** and **New King's School Cadet Corps.**Rec. withdraw from New King's by AO 49/13.

6. Imperial Cadet Yeomanry (City of London): Rec. 28.2.11 (City of London) (AO 161/11). Aff. to HAC by AO 365/21. See also Yorkshire Squadron Imperial Cadet Yeomanry.

7. Imperial Service Cadet Corps, Brighton: Rec. 10.4.11 (Sussex) (AO 130/11) and aff. to 1st Home Counties Brigade RFA. Redes. **1st Cadet Bn.,1st Home Counties Brigade RFA (Imperial Service) Cadet Corps** by AO 49/13. Inc. to eight companies by AO 307/18. Inc. to eleven companies by AO 69/19. Reduced to five companies by AO 150/22. Reduced to four companies by AO 401/22.

8. Imperial Service Cadet Corps, Eastbourne: Rec. 20.4.14 (Sussex) (AO 188/14) and aff. to 2nd Home Counties Brigade RFA.

9. Inns of Court, 1st Cadet Battalion: Rec. 7.12.17 (County of London) (AO 111/18). Disbanded by AO 219/19.

10. Inverness Cadet Battalion, 1st, The Boys Brigade: Rec. 2.5.18 (Inverness) (AO 307/18). Inc. to four companies by AO 226/21.

11. Ipswich Cadet Company, 2nd, The Boys Brigade: Rec. 1.9.21 (Suffolk) (AO 452/21).

12. Irlam and Cadishead Cadet Company: Rec. 4.10.18 (East Lancs) (AO 373/18). Disbanded by AO 61/20.

13. Isles of Scilly Company: See 1st Cadet Bn. of Cornwall.

14. Isles of Scilly Company, Church Lads Brigade: Rec. 28.8.11 (Cornwall) (AO 347/11).

15. Isleworth County School Cadet Company: Rec. 15.3.15 (Middlesex) (AO 139/15) and aff. to 8th Bn. Middlesex Regt. Became part of 2nd Cadet Bn. Middlesex Regt. by AO 96/16.

16. Islington Artillery Cadet Brigade: Rec. 18.7.20 (County of London) (AO 459/20) and aff. to 53rd London Medium Brigade RGA. Disbanded by AO 265/22.

J

1. John Lyon School Cadet Company: Rec. 10.5.15 (Middlesex) (AO 261/15) and aff. to 9th Bn. Middlesex Regt. Became part of 3rd Cadet Bn. Middlesex Regt. by AO 96/16.

2. Judd School (Tonbridge) Cadet Corps: Rec. 31.12.17 (Kent) (AO 111/18) and aff. to 3rd Bn. Kent Volunteer Regt. Absorbed into Kent Public Secondary Schools Cadet Bn. by AO 137/19.

K

1. Kendal Grammar School Cadet Company: Rec. 29.8.17 (Westmoreland) (AO 360/17) and aff. to 4th Bn. Border Regt. Disbanded by AO 493/21.

2. Kensington and Hamersmith Navy League Boys Brigade: Rec. 19.1.12 (County of London) (AO 143/12) and aff. to 13th Bn. London Regt. Disbanded by AO 95/17.

3. Kensington Cadet Corps: Rec. 2.2.11 (County of London) (AO 102/11) and aff. to 2nd London Divisional Royal Engineers. Redes. **Cadet Company, Royal Engineers 2nd London Division (Kensington Cadet Corps)** by AO 249/11. Redes. **Royal Engineers Cadets (2nd London Division)** by AO 373/13. Disbanded by AO 514/20.

4. Kent College (Canterbury) Cadet Corps: Rec. 28.5.15 (Kent) (AO 261/15) and aff. to 4th Bn. East Kent Regt. Absorbed into Kent Public Secondary Schools Cadet Bn. by AO 137/19.

5. Kent (Fortress) Royal Engineers Cadet Battalion: Rec. in AO 121/13 by the amal. of Nos 1 to 4 Cadet Companies, Kent (Fortress) RE. Amal. with 2nd Cadet Bn. Kent (Fortress) RE to form a battalion of twelve companies by AO 111/18. Nos 7, 8 and 9 Companies absorbed into Kent Public Secondary Schools Cadet Bn. by AO 137/19. No 10 Company rec. 24.6.18 (AO 240/18). No 6 Company disbanded by AO 340/19. Admin. by Kent TFA.

6. Kent (Fortress) Royal Engineers, 2nd Cadet Battalion: Rec. 6.11.14 (Kent) (AO 79/15). Amal. with Kent (Fortress) RE Cadet Bn. as a battalion of twelve companies by AO 111/18.

7. Kent (Fortress) Royal Engineers, Nos 1 to 4 Companies: No 1 rec. 1.5.11 (AO 161/11). **No 2** rec. 13.2.12 (AO 207/12). **No 3** rec. 22.5.12 (AO 207/12). **No 4** rec. 11.1.13 (AO 49/13). Amal. as **Kent (Fortress) RE Cadet Bn.** by AO 121/13.

8. Kent Public Secondary Schools Cadet Battalion: Rec. 29.11.18 (AO 137/19) and formed by the amal. of Ashford Grammar School, Kent College, Ramsgate County School, Simon Langton School, Bromley School, Borden Grammar School, Judd School, Cinque Ports (Fortress) RE Cadets and 7th, 8th, 9th Companies of the Kent (Fortress) RE Cadet Bn. Establishment twelve companies and admin. by Kent TFA. Reduced to ten companies by AO 483/22.

9. Kettering Grammar School Cadet Corps: Rec. 30.9.16 (Northampton) (AO 375/16) and aff. to 4th Bn. Northamptonshire Regt.

10. Kidderminster Cadet Company: Rec. 13.4.18 (Worcester) (AO 173/18) and aff. to 1st Volunteer Bn. Worcestershire Regt. Transferred to 7th Bn. by AO 116/20. Disbanded by AO 317/20.

11. Kidderminster Grammar School Cadet Company: See 3rd Cadet Bn. Worcestershire Regt.

12. Kilburn Grammar School Cadet Company: Rec. 10.3.13 (Middlesex) (AO 187/13) and aff. to 9th Bn. Middlesex Regt. Became part of 3rd Cadet Bn. Middlesex Regt. by AO 96/16.

13. Kimbolton Grammar School Cadet Corps: Rec. 8.11.17 (Hunts) (AO 51/18) and aff. to 1st Bn. Huntingdonshire Volunteer Regt. Transferred to Hunts Cyclist Bn. by AO 116/20.

14. **King Edward VI School Cadet Corps, Chelmsford:** See Chelmsford .

15. **King Edward VI School (Nuneaton) Cadet Corps:** Rec. 1.11.15 (Warwick) (AO 457/15). Absorbed into 3rd (Schools) Cadet Bn. Royal Warwickshire Regt. by AO 160/16.

16. **King Edward VI School (Southampton) Cadet Corps:** Rec. 13.12.15 (Southampton) (AO 23/16) and aff. to 5th Bn. Hampshire Regt. Redes. **Southampton, King Edward VI School Cadet Corps** by AO 406/16. Amal. with Tauntons School to form **5th Hampshire Regt. Cadet Bn.** by AO 307/18.

17. **King Edward VI School (Stratford-on-Avon) Cadet Corps:** Rec. 29.1.16 (Warwick) (AO 96/16). Absorbed into 3rd (Schools) Cadet Bn. Royal Warwickshire Regt. by AO 160/16.

18. **King Edward's Grammar School (Aston) Cadet Corps:** Rec. 14.12.14 (Warwick) (AO 79/15). Absorbed into 3rd (Schools) Cadet Bn. Royal Warwickshire Regt. by AO 261/15. Disbanded by AO 265/22.

19. **King Edward's Grammar School (Five Ways) Cadet Corps:** Rec. 15.7.15 (Warwick) (AO 343/15). Became part of 4th (Schools) Cadet Bn. Royal Warwickshire Regt. by AO 160/16.

20. **King Edward's School, Camp Hill Cadet Corps:** Rec. 4.12.14 (Warwick) (AO 41/15). Absorbed into 3rd (Schools) Cadet Bn. Royal Warwickshire Regt. by AO 261/15. Disbanded by AO 310/22.

21. **King Edward's School, Stourbridge Cadet Company:** Rec. 12.2.15 (Worcester) (AO 139/15) and aff. to 7th Bn. Worcestershire Regt. Became part of Worcestershire Cadet Bn. by AO 188/16.

22. **King Edward's School (Witley) Cadet Corps:** Rec. 15.1.12 (Surrey) (AO 41/12).

23. **King's Royal Rifle Corps, 1st Cadet Battalion:** Rec. 1.1.11 (City of London) (AO 65/11). Absorbed St. Anne's School Cadet Company by AO 275/17.

24. **King's School (Chester) Cadet Corps:** Rec. 26.9.15 (Chester) (AO 430/15).

25. **King's School, Ottery St. Mary Cadet Corps:** Rec. 19.6.18 (Devon) (AO 240/18) and aff. to 4th Bn. Devonshire Regt.

26. **King's School (Peterborough) Cadet Corps:** Rec. 22.7.11 (Northampton) (AO 249/11) and aff. to 4th Bn. Northamptonshire Regt. Transferred to 336 (Howitzer) Battery, RFA by AO 25/21.

27. **Kingsbridge Grammar School Cadet Corps:** Rec. 12.12.17 (Devon) (AO 111/18) and aff. to 5th Bn. Devonshire Regt.

28. **Kingston Grammar School Cadet Corps:** Rec. 15.11.15 (Surrey) (AO 457/15) and aff. to 6th Bn. East Surrey Regt. Became part of 1st Cadet Bn. East Surrey Regt. by AO 103/19.

29. **Kingswood Training School Cadet Corps:** Rec. 18.12.17 (Gloucester) (AO 111/18) and aff. to 2nd Bn. City of Bristol Volunteer Regt. Inc. to five companies by AO 69/19.

30. **Kinlochleven Cadet Company:** Rec. 25.7.19 (Argyll) (AO 419/19) and aff. to 8th Bn. Argyll and Sutherland Highlanders. Disbanded by AO 398/21.

31. Kirkby Lonsdale Cadet Company: Rec. 2.3.11 (Westmoreland) (AO 130/11) and aff. to 4th Bn. Border Regt. Disbanded by AO 373/18.

32. Kirkliston Cadet Company, 1st, The Boys Brigade: Rec. 26.5.21 (Linlithgow) (AO 323/21). Transferred to the admin. of Midlothian TAA by AO 229/22.

33. Knightsbridge Imperial Service Cadets, 1st: Rec. 27.4.15 (County of London) (AO 261/15) and aff. to 13th Bn. London Regt. Inc. to three companies by AO 340/19. Disbanded by AO 371/20.

34. Knutsford (Parish) Cadet Company: Rec. 18.10.11 (Chester) (AO 316/11). Rec. withdrawn by AO 61/20.

L

1. Lambeth Cadet Corps, 1st: Rec. by AO 24/20 and formed by the amal. of South London Cadets and 1st Cadet Bn. 10th Bn. County of London Volunteer Regt. Rec. withdrawn by AO 435/22. Admin. by County of London TFA.

2. Lanarkshire Cadet Battalion (Scottish Rifles), 1st: Rec. 17.12.15 (Lanark) (AO 96/16) and aff. to 6th Bn. Cameronians. Uddington Cadet Company formed and added to battalion by AO 168/17. Inc. to six companies by AO 275/17. Inc. to eight companies by AO 360/17. Inc. to fifteen companies by AO 111/18.

3. Lancashire Fusiliers, 8th Bn. 1st Cadet Company: See Broughton Lads Brigade.

4. Lancaster Regt.,King's Own Royal, 1st Cadet Battalion: Rec. 15.2.15 (West Lancs) (AO 225/15) and aff. to 5th Bn. Disbanded by AO 527/21.

5. Larbert Company, 2nd, Boys Brigade Cadets: Rec. 2.5.22 (Stirling) (AO 265/22).

6. Largs Boys Brigade Cadet Company, 1st: Rec. 8.11.17 (Bute) (AO 111/18).

7. Largs Cadet Company: Rec. 7.2.18 (Bute) (AO 149/18) and aff. to the Bute (Mountain) Battery RGA. Rec. withdrawn by AO 493/21.

8. Latymer Upper School (Hammersmith) Cadet Corps: Rec. 21.11.16 (County of London) (AO 65/17) and aff. to 13th Bn. London Regt. Reduced to four companies by AO 310/22.

9. Lawe Cadet Company: Rec. 14.11.18 (Durham) (AO 69/19).

10. Leamington Municipal School Cadet Corps: Rec. 18.2.15 (Warwick) (AO 139/15). Absorbed into 3rd Cadet Bn. Royal Warwickshire Regt. by AO 261/15.

11. Leeds Cadet Company, 13th, The Boys Brigade: Rec. 8.9.22 (West Yorks) (AO 401/22).

12. Leeds Cadet Unit, Catholic Boys Brigade: Rec. 10.6.13 (West Yorks) (AO 274/13). Disbanded by AO 156/20.

13. Leeds Modern School Cadet Corps: Rec. 23.2.15 (West Yorks) (AO 139/15). Aff. to 8th Bn. West Yorkshire Regt. by AO 24/20. Disbanded by AO 435/22.

14. Leeds Postal Telegraph Messengers Cadet Company: Rec. 30.1.11 (West Yorks) (AO 65/11) and aff. to 7th Bn. West Yorkshire Regt. Transferred to Northern Telegraph Companies, Royal Engineers by AO 86/13.

15. Leeds Volunteer Cadet Battalion: Rec. 1.7.18 (West Yorks) (AO 307/18) and aff. to Leeds Group West Riding Volunteers. Transferred to 8th Bn. West Yorkshire Regt. by AO 116/20.

16. Leicestershire Regt., 1st Cadet Battalion: Rec. 19.5.15 (Leicester) (AO 225/15) and aff. to 4th Bn.

17. Leigh Grammar School Cadet Corps: Rec. 4.2.16 (East Yorks) (AO 96/16) and aff. to 5th Bn. Manchester Regt. Disbanded by AO 378/18.

18. Leigh-on-Sea Company, 1st, The Boys Brigade Cadets: Rec. 30.4.19 (Essex) (AO 251/19).

19. Leinster House (Putney) Cadets: Rec. 8.2.15 (County of London) (AO 139/15) and aff. to 15th Bn. London Regt. Inc. to two companies by AO 310/22.

20. Leominster Cadet Company, Church Lads Brigade: Rec. 13.4.22 (Hereford) (AO 265/22).

21. Lewisham Cadet Battalion: Rec. 30.5.13 (City of London) (AO 235/13). Aff. to 4th London (Howitzer) Brigade RFA by AO 139/15. Transferred to 20th Bn. London Regt. by AO 342/18. Amal. with West Lewisham Cadet Corps to form **1st Cadet Bn. (Lewisham), 20th Bn. London Regt.** by A.O. 323/21. Reduced to four companies by AO 198/22.

22. Lewis School (Pengam) Cadet Corps: Rec. 18.11.15 (Glamorgan) (AO 23/16). Aff. to 5th Bn. Welsh Regt. by A.O. 125/16. Disbanded by AO 265/22.

23. Leytonstone and Leyton County High School Cadet Corps: See Leytonstone County High School.

24. Leytonstone County High School Cadet Corps: Rec. 29.9.15 (Essex) (AO 430/15) and aff. to 7th Bn. Essex Regt. Redes. **Leytonstone and Leyton County High School** by AO 188/16. Became part of 5th (Schools) Cadet Bn. Essex Regt. by AO 335/16.

25. Lichfield Cadet Battalion, 1st, Church Lads Brigade: Rec. 7.11.11 (Stafford) (AO 75/12).

26. Lichfield Cadet Battalion, 3rd, Church Lads Brigade: Rec. 24.5.12 (Stafford) (AO 233/12).

27. Lichfield Cadet Battalion, 5th, Church Lads Brigade: Rec. 6.8.11 (Stafford) (AO 75/12).

28. Lichfield Cadet Battalion, 7th, Church Lads Brigade: Rec. 15.8.11 (Stafford) (AO 75/12).

29. Lincoln Cadet Battalion, 3rd: No 1 (Church of England Men's Society) Company rec. 17.1.13 (AO 86/13). **No 2 (Stamford School)** Company rec. 11.10.15 (AO 457/15). Aff. to 4th Bn. Lincolnshire Regt. by AO 25/21. **No 3 (Grimsby and Cleethorpes)** Company rec. 14.10.15 (AO 188/16). Disbanded by AO 265/22. Battalion admin. by Lincoln TFA.

30. Lincoln Cadet Battalion, 4th: Rec. 19.7.18 (Lincoln) (AO 307/18) and aff. to 4th Volunteer Bn. Lincolnshire Regt. **No 3 (Hykeham) Company** rec. 10.8.18 (AO 342/18). Aff. transferred to 4th Bn. Lincolnshire Regt. by AO 116/20. Disbanded by AO 265/22.

31. Lincoln Cadet Battalion, 1st, Church Lads Brigade: No 1 (St. Nicholas) Company rec. 22.9.11 (AO 347/11). **No 2 Company** rec. 7.10.13 (AO 398/13). **Nos 3 and 4 Companies** rec. 6.1.15 (AO 139/15). Battalion admin. by Lincoln TFA.

32. Lincoln Cadet Battalion, 2nd, Church Lads Brigade: Rec. 21.5.12 (Lincoln) (AO 233/12).

33. Lincoln School Cadet Corps: Rec. 9.5.16 (Lincoln) (AO 188/16) and aff. to 4th Bn. Lincolnshire Regt.

34. Liscard High School Cadet Corps: Rec. 14.11.14 (Chester) (AO 41/15) and aff. to 4th Bn. Cheshire Regt.

35. Little Mill Cadet Company: See 3rd Cadet Bn. Monmouthshire Regt.

36. Liverpool Cadet Battalion, 6th, The Boys Brigade. Rec. 19.8.18 (West Lancs) (AO 307/18). Inc. to eight companies by AO 514/20.

37. Liverpool Cadet Battalion, 7th, The Boys Brigade: Rec. 22.10.20 (West Lancs) (AO 514/20).

38. Liverpool Cadet Battalion, 1st, Church Lads Brigade: Rec. 6.10.11 (East Lancs) (AO 41/12). Inc. to six companies by AO 51/18. Reduced to four companies by AO 95/22. Reduced to three companies by AO 401/22.

39. Liverpool Cadet Battalion, 2nd, Church Lads Brigade: Rec. 29.5.12 (West Lancs) (AO 207/12).

40. Liverpool Cadet Battalion, 3rd, Church Lads Brigade: Rec. 26.6.12 (West Lancs) (AO 233/12).

41. Liverpool Cadet Battalion, 4th, Church Lads Brigade: Rec. 12.6.18 (West Lancs) (AO 240/18).

42. Liverpool, City of, Cadet Battalion The King's Liverpool Regt: Rec. 1.12.11 (West Lancs) (AO 320/12) and aff. to Liverpool Infantry Brigade. Aff. to 5th Bn. King's Liverpool Regt. by AO 514/20.

43. Liverpool Church Cadet Battalion: Rec. 30.10.14 (West Lancs) (AO 225/15). Redes. **5th Cadet Bn. King's Liverpool Regt.** by AO 240/18. See also Alsop High School Cadet corps.

44. Liverpool Collegiate School Cadet Corps: Rec. 20.11.15 (West Lancs) (AO 23/16). Aff. to 6th Bn. King's Liverpool Regt. by AO 62/16.

45. Liverpool Company, Jewish Lads Brigade: Rec. 22.4.15 (West Lancs) (AO 23/16). Disbanded by AO 265/22.

46. Liverpool Regt.,King's, 1st Territorial Cadet Battalion: Rec. 19.7.10 (West Lancs) (AO 11/11) and aff. to Liverpool Infantry Brigade. Rec. withdrawn by AO 290/12.

47. Liverpool Regt.,King's, 5th Cadet Battalion: See Liverpool Church Cadet Bn. and Alsop High School.

48. Liverpool Regt.,King's, City of Liverpool Cadet Battalion: See City of Liverpool Cadet Bn.

49. Llandaff Cadet Battalion, 1st, Church Lads Brigade: Rec. 3.4.12 (Glamorgan) (AO 143/12). Inc. to eight companies by AO 251/19.

50. Llandaff Cadet Battalion, 2nd, Church Lads Brigade: Rec. 6.7.12 (Glamorgan) (AO 233/12).

51. Llandaff Cadet Battalion, 3rd, Church Lads Brigade: Rec. 6.7.12 (Glamorgan) (AO 233/12). Absorbed St. Gwlady's, Bargoed Company CLB by AO 144/14. Disbanded by AO 452/21.

52. Llandaff Cadet Corps, 9th, Church Lads Brigade: Rec. 15.7.12 (Monmouth) (AO 260/12). Redes. **1st Monmouth Cadet Bn. CLB** and inc. to five companies by AO 401/22. Inc. to six companies by AO 29/23.

53. Llanrwst County School Cadet Corps: Rec. 19.10.16 (Denbigh) (AO 406/16) and aff. to 4th Bn. Royal Welsh Fusiliers. Disbanded by AO 452/21.

54. Logie Boys Brigade Cadet Company: Rec. 2.5.22 (Stirling) (AO 310/22).

55. London Cadet Battalions, The Boys Brigade: 1st to 10th rec. 18.4.17 (AO 168/17). 4th reduced to three companies by AO 198/22. 9th inc. to six companies by AO 310/22. 10th inc. to seven companies by AO 310/22. 11th rec. 28.6.17 (AO 275/17). Inc. to five companies by AO 365/21. All battalions admin. by County of London TFA.

56. London Cadet Battalion, 1st, Jewish Lads Brigade: Rec. 1.4.15 (City of London) (AO 225/15). Inc. to sixteen companies by AO 111/18. Inc. to seventeen companies by AO 276/19. Inc. to nineteen companies by AO 406/20. Inc. to twenty-one companies by AO 265/22. Reduced to fifteen companies by AO 401/22. Reduced to thirteen companies by AO 483/22.

57. London Cadet Battalion, 2nd, Jewish Lads Brigade: Rec. 7.6.22 (City of London) (AO 401/22). Reduced to nine companies by AO 483/22.

58. London Cadet Battalions, (London Diocesan Church Lads Brigade): 1st to 12th rec. 12.3.12 (AO 207/12). 13th rec. 12.3.12. 14th rec. 12.3.12 (AO 156/13). All battalions admin. by County of London TFA. 5th to 12th Cadet Battalions the Middlesex Regt. (London Diocesan Church Lads Brigade) transfered to the admin. of the County of London TFA and together with London Battalions reorganised by AO 211/20 as **Cadet Battalions, London Division CLB.** The reorganisation went as follows:-**1st Bn.** (late 5th CB Middx. Regt.). Reduced to seven companies by AO 95/22. Reduced to six companies by AO 310/22. **2nd Bn.** (late 2nd London Bn.). Reduced to three companies by AO 95/22. Reduced to two companies by AO 310/22. **3rd Bn.** (late 6th CB Middx. Regt.). Reduced to nine companies by AO 95/22. Reduced to eight companies by AO 310/22. **4th Bn.** (late 12th CB Middx. Regt.). **5th Bn.** (late 1st London Bn.). Reduced to five companies by AO 95/22. Reduced to two companies by AO 310/22. **6th Bn.** (late 6th London Bn.). Reduced to five companies by AO 95/22. Reduced to two companies by AO 310/22. **7th Bn.** (late 8th CB Middx. Regt.). Reduced to eight companies by AO 310/22. **8th Bn.** (late 9th CB Middx. Regt.). Reduced to five companies by AO 310/22. **9th Bn.** (late 9th London Bn.). Reduced to seven companies by AO 310/22. **10th Bn.** (late 10th London Bn.). Reduced to three companies by AO 310/22. **11th Bn.** (late 5th London Bn.). Reduced to seven companies by AO 310/22. **12th Bn.** (late 4th London Bn.). Reduced to four companies by AO 95/22. Reduced to two companies by AO 310/22. **13th Bn.** (late 3rd London Bn.). Reduced to eight companies by AO

310/22. **14th Bn.** (late 10th CB Middx. Regt.). Reduced to five companies by AO 95/22. **15th Bn.** (late 11th CB Middx. Regt.). Reduced to six companies by AO 95/22. Reduced to five companies by AO 310/22. **16th Bn.** (late 7th London Bn.). Reduced to five companies by AO 95/22. Reduced to four companies by AO 310/22. **17th Bn.** (late 8th London Bn.). Reduced to six companies by AO 310/22. **18th Bn.** (late 7th CB Middx. Regt.).

59. London, City of, Brigade, Royal Field Artillery Cadet Corps: Rec. 4.2.19 (City of London) (AO 219/19). Disbanded by AO 310/22.

60. London, City of, 1st Cadet Battalion: See Lord Robert's Boys.

61. London, City of, 2nd Cadet Battalion (Secondary Schools): Rec. 10.10.11 (City of London) (AO 229/16) and formed by the amal. of Coopers' Company's Cadet Corps and Parmiter's School Cadet Corps. Aff. to 5th Bn. London Regt.

62. London, City of, 3rd Cadet Battalion: Rec. by AO 275/17 and formed by the amal. of George Green's School and Raines School cadet units. Inc. to four companies by AO 373/18. Admin. by City of London TFA.

63. London, City of, Royal Engineers Training Corps: Rec. 6.7.17 (City of London) (AO 275/17). Inc. to four companies by AO 251/19.

64. London, County of, 1st Royal Engineers Cadets (Woolwich): See 1st Woolwich Cadet Corps.

65. London, 1st, 56th Divisional Engineers Cadets: Rec. 1.2.22 (County of London) (AO 265/22).

66. London, 2nd Division Royal Engineers Cadet Company: See Kensington Cadet Corps.

67. London Regt.,1st Cadet Battalion (The Queen's): See 1st Cadet Bn. Royal West Surrey Regt.

68. London Regt.,2nd (Civil Service) Cadet Battalion: See Civil Service Cadet Corps.

69. London Regt.,3rd Battalion Cadet Corps: See 1st North Paddington Cadets.

70. London Regt.,3rd Cadet Battalion: Rec. 20.7.16 (County of London) (AO 302/16) and aff. to 23rd Bn. Inc. to eight companies by AO 251/19.

71. London Regt.,1st Cadet Battalion, 4th Battalion: Rec. by AO 156/20 and formed by the amal. of South West London, St. Christopher's and Stanhope Institute cadet units. Reduced to four companies by AO 198/22. Admin. by City of London TFA.

72. London Regt.,1st Cadet Company, 6th Battalion: Rec. 15.2.11 (City of London) (AO 161/11).

73. London Regt.,1st and 2nd Cadet Companies, 7th Battalion: Rec. 4.5.15 (City of London) (AO 225/15). Redes. **7th Bn. London Regt. Cadet Corps** by AO 188/16. Inc. to eight companies by AO 51/18. Inc. to eleven companies by AO 149/18. Inc. to fourteen companies by AO 173/18. Inc. to fifteen companies by AO 307/18. Redes. **1st Cadet Bn. 7th Bn. London Regt.** by AO 219/19. Redes. **7th London Detachment, 1st Cadet Bn. Royal Fusiliers** by AO 483/22.

74. London Regt.,10th Battalion Cadet Corps: Rec. 4.2.14 (County of London) (AO 416/14). Inc. to eight companies by AO 340/19. Reduced to two companies by AO 198/22.

75. London Regt.,19th Battalion Cadet Corps: See St. Pancras Cadet Corps.

76. London Regt.,1st Cadet Battalion, 20th Battalion: See Lewisham Cadet Bn.

77. London Regt.,23rd Battalion Cadet Corps: Rec. 13.10.21 (County of London) (AO 493/21).

78. London Scottish Cadet Corps: Rec. 19.4.17 (County of London) (AO 275/17) and aff. to 14th Bn. London Regt. Inc. to eight companies by AO 340/19. Rec. withdrawn by AO 435/22.

79. London Volunteer Regt.,1st Cadet Battalion, 10th Battalion: Rec. 6.5.18 (County of London) (AO 209/18). Amal. with South London Cadets to form **1st Bn. Lambeth Cadet Corps** by AO 24/20.

80. London Volunteer Regt.,1st Cadet Battalion, 14th Battalion: Rec. 6.12.17 (County of London) (AO 149/18). Redes. **1st Bn. Battersea Cadet Corps** and aff. to 23rd Bn. London Regt. by AO 24/20. Disbanded by AO 493/21.

81. London Volunteer Regt.,1st Cadet Battalion, 15th Battalion: Rec. 7.2.18 (County of London) (AO 149/18). Transferred to the admin. of Surrey TFA and redes. **2nd (Streatham) Cadet Bn. East Surrey Regt.** by AO 255/20. Reduced to one company by AO 150/22.

82. London Volunteer Regt.,2nd Cadet Battalion, 15th Battalion: Rec. 24.4.18 (County of London) (AO 209/18). Disbanded by AO 116/20.

83. London Volunteer Regt.,1st Cadet Battalion, 17th Battalion: Rec. 6.3.18 (County of London) (AO 173/18). Inc. to six companies by AO 340/19. Redes. **West Lewisham Cadet Corps** by AO 24/20. Aff. to 20th Bn. London Regt. by AO 61/20. Amal. with Lewisham Cadet Bn. as **1st Cadet Bn. (Lewisham), 20th London Regt.** by AO 323/21 and admin. transfered to City of London TFA.

84. London Volunteer Regt.,20th Battalion Cadet Corps: Rec. 7.12.17 (County of London) (AO 111/18). Disbanded by AO 116/20.

85. Lord Mayor's Own (Bristol) Cadet Corps: Rec. 18.3.18 (Gloucester) (AO 149/18) and aff. to 1st City of Bristol Volunteer Regt. Disbanded by AO 265/22.

86. Lord Robert's Boys: Rec. 1.1.11 (City of London) (AO 65/11). Redes. **1st City of London Cadet Battalion (Lord Robert's Boys)** by AO 316/11. Reduced to one company and redes. **Lord Robert's Boys Detachment, 1st Cadet Bn. Royal Fusiliers** by AO 483/22.

87. Lord William's Grammar School, Thame Cadet Corps: Rec. 29.1.16 (Oxford) (AO 96/16) and aff. to 4th Bn. Oxfordshire and Buckinghamshire Light Infantry.

88. Loughton School Cadet Corps: Rec. 15.6.15 (Essex) (AO 261/15) and aff. to 4th Bn. Essex Regt. Became part of 5th (Schools) Cadet Bn. Essex Regt. by AO 335/16. Order cancelled by AO 406/16.

89. Lowerstoft Cadet Company, 2nd, The Boys Brigade: Rec. 1.3.21 (Suffolk) (AO 118/21).

90. Lowerstoft Cadet Company, 3rd, The Boys Brigade: Rec. 1.2.21 (Suffolk) (AO 72/21).

91. Ludlow Cadet Company, Church Lads Brigade: See 1st Hereford Cadet Bn. CLB.

92. Luton Modern School Cadet Corps: Rec. 31.5.18 (Bedford) (AO 31/19) and aff. to East Anglian Divisional Engineers. Disbanded by AO 25/21.

93. Lymington Cadet Corps: Rec. 17.3.11 (Southampton) (AO 102/11) and aff. to 7th Bn. Hampshire Regt.

M

1. Macclesfield Grammar School Cadet Corps: Rec. 10.2.14 (Chester) (AO 63/14) and aff. to 7th Bn. Cheshire Regt.

2. Macclesfield Industrial School Cadet Corps: Rec. 27.5.11 (Chester) (AO 191/11) and aff. to 7th Bn. Cheshire Regt. Rec. withdrawn by AO 360/17.

3. Magdalen College School Cadet Corps: Rec. 26.4.19 (Oxford) (AO 276/19) and aff. to 4th Bn. Oxfordshire and Buckinghamshire Light Infantry.

4. Magdalen College School, Brackley Cadet Corps: Rec. 7.5.15 (Northampton) (AO 225/15) and aff. to 4th Bn. Northamptonshire Regt.

5. Magdalene Cadet Company: Rec. 17.4.12 (City of London) (AO 177/12).

6. Magnus Grammar School Cadet Corps: See 2nd Cadet Bn. Notts and Derby Regt.

7. Maidenhead Cadet Companies: See 1st Cadet Company Royal Berkshire Regt.

8. Maidenhead Town Cadet Company: Rec. 3.5.18 (Berks) (AO 209/18) and aff. to 1st Bn. Berkshire Volunteer Regt. Disbanded by AO 493/21.

9. Maldon Grammar School Cadet Corps: Rec. 14.11.17 (Essex) (AO 51/18) and aff. to 1/2nd Essex Volunteer Regt. Transferred to 5th Bn. Essex Regt. by AO 116/20.

10. Mall School Cadet Company: Rec. 22.12.14 (Middlesex) (AO 79/15) and aff. to 8th Bn. Middlesex Regt. Became part of 2nd Cadet Bn. Middlesex Regt. by AO 96/16.

11. Manchester Cadet Battalions, Church Lads Brigade: 1st rec. 7.3.13 (AO 235/13). Inc. to sixteen companies by AO 307/18. Reduced to eight companies by AO 435/22. **2nd** rec. 13.4.17 (AO 275/17). Absorbed St. Cyprian's Kirkmanshulme and St. Mark's, West Gorton Cadet Companies CLB upon formation. Inc. to ten companies by AO 419/19. Reduced to five companies by AO 95/22. **3rd** rec. 26.8.15 (AO 23/16). **4th** rec. 5.2.15 (AO 109/15). Inc. to nine companies by AO 51/18. Reduced to four companies by AO 419/19. **5th** rec. 5.11.15 (AO 457/15). Absorbed Patricroft Parish Cadet Company CLB upon formation. Reduced to four companies by AO 95/22. **6th** see St. Margaret, Whalley Range and St. Clement's, Urmston Cadet Corps CLB. **7th** rec. 4.10.12 (AO 320/12). Inc. to sixteen companies by AO 137/19. Reduced to thirteen companies by AO 459/20. Reduced to twelve companies by AO 150/22. **8th** rec. 4.6.15 (AO 302/15). Reduced to four companies by AO 435/22. **11th** rec. 4.2.21 (AO 72/21). Absorbed St. Matthew's (Preston), St. Paul's (Farrington) and St. Paul's (Longridge) Cadet Companies CLB upon formation. **12th** rec. 1.11.12 (AO 343/12). **13th** rec. 6.8.20 (AO 459/20). The 3rd and 11th Battalions admin. by West Lancs TFA. All others by East Lancs.

12. Manchester Cadet Companies, The Boys Brigade: 7th rec. 10.8.20 (AO 459/20). 11th rec. 22.8.19 (AO 340/19). 14th rec. 22.8.19 (AO 381/19). 23rd rec. 11.4.19 (AO 219/19). 27th rec. 10.8.20 (AO 459/20). 41st rec. 22.7.20 (AO 459/20). 52nd rec. 28.7.20 (AO 459/20). All units admin. by East Lancs TFA.

13. Manchester Companies, Jewish Lads Brigade: Rec. 7.5.15 (East Lancs) (AO 302/15). Redes. **1st Manchester Cadet Bn. Jewish Lads Brigade** by AO 340/19. Aff. to 8th Bn. Lancashire Fusiliers by AO 95/22.

14. Manchester Regt.,1st Territorial Cadet Battalion: Rec. 6.1.11 (East Lancs) (AO 40/11) and aff. to Manchester Infantry Brigade.

15. Manchester Regt.,2nd Cadet Battalion: See 1st (Coldhurst) Oldham Cadet Corps.

16. Manchester Royal Engineers Cadet Corps: Rec. 7.10.21 (East Lancs) (AO 493/21).

17. "M" and "C", Royal Engineers, 1st Cadet Company: Rec. 19.6.18 (City of Glasgow) (AO 240/18).

18. Manningtree Cadet Company, 1st, The Boys Brigade: Rec. 6.12.20 (Essex) (AO 25/21).

19. Manor House School (Clapham) Cadet Corps: Rec. 19.2.15 (County of London) (AO 139/15). Transferred to the admin. of City of London TFA by AO 149/18. Aff. to 4th Bn. London Regt. by AO 371/20. Disbanded by AO 483/22.

20. Manor Park Cadet Company: Rec. 4.1.11 (Essex) (AO 40/11) and aff. to 4th Bn. Essex Regt. Redes. **2nd Cadet Bn. Essex Regt.** by AO 225/15. Reduced to one company by AO 150/22.

21. Marazion Cadet Company, Church Lads Brigade: Rec. 28.4.16 (Cornwall) (AO 188/16). Disbanded by AO 493/21.

22. March Grammar School Cadet Corps: Rec. 1.4.16 (Cambs and Ely) (AO 160/16) and aff. to 1st Bn. Cambridgeshire Regt. Rec. withdrawn by AO 435/22.

23. Marines, Royal Cadets: See Depot, Royal Marine Cadet Corps.

24. Marling School (Stroud) Cadet Corps: Rec. 18.9.16 (Gloucester) (AO 406/16) and aff. to 5th Bn. Gloucestershire Regt. Inc. to three companies by AO 69/19.

25. Marner School (LCC) Cadet Company: Rec. 13.3.12 (City of London) (AO 177/12). Absorbed into Tower Hamlets Cadets by AO 188/16.

26. Mayfield College School Cadet Corps: Rec. 10.10.21 (Sussex) (AO 527/21) and aff. to 5th Bn. Royal Sussex Regt.

27. Melton Constable Cadet Company, Church Lads Brigade: Rec. 27.3.15 (Norfolk) (AO 225/15). Absorbed into 1st Norwich Cadet Corps, CLB by AO 360/17.

28. Mercer's School Cadet Corps: Rec. 4.5.15 (City of London) (AO 225/15).

29. Merchant Taylors School (Crosby) Cadet Corps: Rec. 12.2.15 (West Lancs) (AO 225/15) and aff. to 6th Bn. King's Liverpool Regt.

30. Merchant Venturers' (Bristol) School Cadet Corps: Rec. 22.3.15 (Gloucester) (AO 225/15) and aff. to 4th Bn. Gloucestershire Regt. Redes. **Cotham Secondary School Cadet Corps** and transfered to South Midland Royal Engineers by AO 156/20.

31. Merrywood School (Bristol) Cadet Unit: Rec. 21.6.15 (Gloucester) (AO 302/15) and aff. to 4th Bn. Gloucestershire Regt. Disbanded by AO 265/22.

32. Middle Docks Cadet Corps: Rec. 9.12.18 (Durham) (AO 69/19) and aff. to 4th Northumbrian (Howitzer) Brigade RFA.

33. Middlesex Regt.,1st Cadet Battalion: Rec. 12.7.15 (Middlesex) (AO 96/16) and formed by the amal. of Tollington School, Christ's College ,Harringay, Friern Barnet School, Enfield Grammar School and Stationers' Company's School cadet units. Aff. to 7th Bn. Inc. to fourteen companies by AO 51/18. Inc. to fifteen companies by AO 111/18. Reduced to five companies by AO 459/20. Reduced to three companies by AO 435/22.

34. Middlesex Regt.,2nd Cadet Battalion: Rec. 12.7.15 (Middlesex) (AO 96/16) and formed by the amal. of Ealing, Ealing County School, Mall School, Southall County School and Isleworth County School cadet units. Aff. to 8th Bn. Reduced to four companies by AO 435/22.

35. Middlesex Regt.,2/2nd Cadet Battalion (Schools): Rec. 14.8.18 (Middlesex) (AO 137/19) and aff. to 8th Bn. Reduced to seven companies by AO 459/20. Reduced to six companies by AO 25/21. Reduced to four companies by AO 150/22. Reduced to three companies by AO 435/22.

36. Middlesex Regt.,3rd Cadet Battalion: Rec. 12.7.15 (Middlesex) (AO 96/16) and formed by the amal. of Harrow, Sudbury House School, Kilburn Grammar School, Brondesbury College and John Lyon School cadet units. Aff. to 9th Bn. Inc. to seven companies by AO 116/20. Reduced to six companies by AO 459/20. Disbanded by AO 452/21.

37. Middlesex Regt.,No 1 Company, 3rd Cadet Battalion: Rec. 24.4.22 (Middlesex) (AO 310/22) and aff. to 9th Bn.

38. Middlesex Regt.,4th Cadet Battalion: Rec. 12.7.15 (Middlesex) (AO 96/16) and formed by the amal. of Bedford Park and Acton cadet units. Aff. to 10th Bn. Inc. to nine companies by AO 111/18. Reduced to five companies by AO 435/22.

39. Middlesex Regt.,5th Cadet Battalion (Schools): Rec. 14.8.18 (Middlesex) (AO 137/19) and aff. to 7th Bn. Inc. to seven companies by AO 219/19. Reduced to six companies by AO 340/19. Reduced to three companies by AO 459/20.

40. Middlesex Regt.,6th Cadet Battalion (Acton): Rec. 27.2.22 (Middlesex) (AO 265/22).

41. Middlesex Regt.,5th to 14th Cadet Battalions (London Diocesan Church Lads Brigade): All rec. 11.5.11 (Middlesex) (AO 284/11). 5th inc. to eight companies by AO 276/19. 7th absorbed 8th by AO 276/19. 8th reduced to ten companies by AO 276/19. 10th reduced to seven companies by AO 276/19. 11th inc. to ten companies by AO 276/19. 12th reduced to six companies by AO 276/19. 14th redes **7th Middlesex Cadet Bn. Church Lads Brigade** and inc to seven companies by AO 276/19. All units later designated as **Church Cadet Brigades of the Diocesan of London.** All units designated **Church Lads Brigade Cadets, London Division** by AO 61/20. 5th to 12th transfered to admin. of County of London TFA by AO 116/20.

42. Midhurst Grammar School Cadet Corps: Rec. 22.10.18 (Sussex) (AO 103/19) and aff. to 4th Bn. Royal Sussex Regt.

43. Mid-Suffolk Cadet Battalion, The Boys Brigade: See 1st Stowmarket Cadet Company BB.

44. Millerston Cadet Company, 1st, The Boys Brigade: Rec. 26.5.21 (Lanark) (AO 271/21). Inc. to two companies by AO 265/22.

45. Millfield Platoon (St Joseph's) Catholic Cadets: Rec. 17.9.20 (Durham) (AO 555/20). Disbanded by AO 493/21.

46. Milngavie Cadet Company, 1st, The Boys Brigade: Rec. 25.3.19 (Dumbarton) (AO 251/19).

47. Mirfield Company, 2nd, Boys Brigade Cadets: Rec. 27.7.18 (West Yorks) (AO 307/18).

48. Moffat Cadet Corps: Rec. 10.1.18 (Dumfries) (AO 149/18) and aff. to 5th Bn. King's Own Scottish Borderers.

49. Mold County School Cadet Corps: Rec. 22.6.16 (Flint) (AO 302/16) and aff. to 5th Bn. Royal Welsh Fusiliers. Became part of 1st Cadet Bn. 5th Bn. Royal Welsh Fusiliers by AO 240/18.

50. Monkwearmouth Platoon (St. Benet's) Catholic Cadets: Rec. 24.8.20 (Durham) (AO 555/20).

51. Monmouth Cadet Battalion, 1st, Church Lads Brigade: See 9th Llandaff Cadet Corps CLB.

52. Monmouth Grammar School Cadet Corps: Rec. 15.3.11 (Monmouth) (AO 130/11) and aff. to 2nd Bn. Monmouthshire Regt. Became part of 1st Cadet Bn. Monmouthshire Regt. by AO 233/12.

53. Monmouthshire Regt.,1st Cadet Battalion: Formed (AO 233/12) by the amal. of Usk, Chepstow, Abercarn, Ebbw Vale, Monmouth Grammar School and Abergavenny cadet units. Aff. to 1st Bn. Monmouthshire Regt. by AO 160/16. **Risca and Cross Keys Cadet Corps** formed and added to battalion by AO 229/16. **Caldicot Cadet Company** formed and added by AO 168/17. Inc. to seven companies by AO 209/18. Admin. by Monmouth TFA.

54. Monmouthshire Regt.,2nd Cadet Battalion: Rec. 25.8.15 (Monmouth) (AO 381/15) and aff. to 1st Bn. Monmouthshire Regt. Transfered to 2nd Bn. by AO 160/16. Reduced to three companies by AO 401/22.

55. Monmouthshire Regt.,3rd Cadet Battalion: Rec. 21.3.16 (Monmouth) (AO 160/16) and aff. to 3rd Bn. Monmouthshire Regt. **Brynmawr and Beaufort Cadet Company** formed and added by AO 375/16. **Cwn and Little Mill Companies** formed and added by AO 51/18. Inc. to ten companies by AO 51/18. Reduced to two companies by AO 401/22.

56. Monmouthshire Regt.,4th Cadet Battalion: Rec. 1.1.18 (Monmouth) (AO 149/18) and aff. to 3rd Bn. Monmouthshire Regt.

57. Monoux Grammar School Cadet Corps, Walthamstow: Rec. 9.5.17 (Essex) (AO 275/17) and aff. to 7th Bn. Essex Regt. Disbanded by AO 527/21.

58. Morpeth Cadet Company, 1st, The Boys Brigade: Rec. 3.5.18 (Northumberland) (AO 240/18). Rec. withdrawn by AO 527/21.

59. Morpeth Grammar School Cadet Company: Rec. 26.10.10 (Northumberland) (AO 309/10) and aff. to 7th Bn. Northumberland Fusiliers.

60. Mountain Ash County School Cadet Corps: Rec. 21.3.18 (Glamorgan) (AO 173/18). Disbanded by AO 452/21.

61. Mount St. Mary's College (Chesterfield) Cadet Corps: Rec. 27.6.15 (Derby) (AO 302/15). Absorbed into the Derbyshire Schools Cadet Battalion by AO 219/19.

62. M.S.W. Cadet Company, 2nd, The Black Watch: Rec. 18.5.20 (City of Dundee) (AO 371/20) and aff. to 4th Bn.

N

1. Nantwich Cadet Corps: Rec. 23.11.17 (Chester) (AO 51/18) and aff. to 4th Bn. Cheshire Volunteer Regt. Aff. transferred to 7th Bn. Cheshire Regt. by AO 116/20. Disbanded by AO 265/22.

2. Neath Intermeadiat School Cadet Corps: Rec. 7.11.16 (Glamorgan) (AO 406/16) and aff. to 6th Bn. Welsh Regt. Disbanded by AO 156/20.

3. New Brighton Cadet Corps, 1st: Rec. 5.7.11 (Chester) (AO 220/11). Rec. withdrawn by AO 381/19.

4. New Brighton Cadet Corps, 2nd: Rec. 28.9.14 (Chester) (AO 511/14) and aff. to 4th Bn. Cheshire Regt. Rec. withdrawn by AO 381/19.

5. New Brighton Cadet Corps, 3rd: Rec. 5.10.14 (Chester) (AO 511/14) and aff. to 4th Bn. Cheshire Regt. Inc. to two companies by AO 381/19. Redes. **Wallasey Cadet Corps** by AO 61/20. Disbanded by AO 459/20.

6. Newcastle Cadet Battalion, Church Lads Brigade: Rec. 2.8.12 (Northumberland) (AO 260/12).

7. Newcastle Modern School Cadets: Rec. 6.8.15 (Northumberland) (AO 381/15) and aff. to Northumbrian Divisional Engineers.

8. Newcastle-on-Tyne Cadet Battalion, The Boys Brigade: Rec. 2.11.17 (Northumberland) (AO 51/18). Inc. to eight companies by AO 209/18.

9. New College (Hern Bay) Cadet Corps: Rec. 4.11.10 (Kent) (AO 65/11) and aff. to 4th Bn. East Kent Regt. Amal. with Herne Bay College Cadet Corps by AO 95/17.

10. New King School (LCC) Cadet Corps: Rec. 31.3.11 (City of London) (AO 177/12). See 2nd (Fulham) Bn. Imperial Cadet Corps.

11. Newport Market School Cadet Corps: Rec. 17.10.11 (County of London) (AO 11/12).

12. Newport Territorial Cadet Battalion: Rec. 1.3.11 (Monmouth) (AO 102/11) and aff. to 4th Welsh Brigade RFA. 2nd and 3rd Batteries rec. 26.4.11 (AO 161/11). Inc. to five batteries by AO 452/21.

13. Newton Abbot Cadet Corps: See Hayton (Newton Abbot) Cadet Corps.

14. Newton Abbot Secondary School Cadet Corps: Rec. 13.3.18 (Devon) (AO 173/18) and aff. to 5th Bn. Devonshire Regt.

15. Newton College Cadet Corps: Rec. 3.8.15 (Devon) (AO 343/15) and aff. to 5th Bn. Devonshire Regt.

16. Newton Stewart Company, The Boys Brigade: Rec. 1.3.18 (Wigtown) (AO 149/18).

17. Newtown County School Cadet Unit: Rec. 11.12.17 (Montgomery) (AO 111/18) and aff. to 1st Bn. Montgomeryshire Volunteer Regt. Rec. withdrawn by AO 24/20. Note: This unit seems to have been re-recognised as **1st Cadet (Newtown County School) Company, 7th Bn. Royal Welsh Fusiliers.**

18. Norfolk Artillery Cadets: See Cadet Norfolk Artillery.

19. Norfolk Volunteer Cadet Corps, 1st: Rec. 27.3.18 (Norfolk) (AO 173/18) and aff. to 1st Volunteer Bn. Norfolk Regt. Absorbed into the Cadet Norfolk Artillery 16.7.19 (AO 419/19).

20. Northampton Cadet Battalion, 1st, The Boys Brigade: Rec. 1.7.18 (Northampton) (AO 307/18). Inc. to eight companies by AO 276/19. Inc. to nine companies by AO 371/20.

21. Northampton School Cadet Corps: Rec. 6.2.14 (Northampton) (AO 63/14) and aff. to 4th Bn. Northamptonshire Regt.

22. North Berwick Cadet Corps: Rec. 6.6.10 (Haddington) (AO 258/10) and aff. to 8th Bn. Royal Scots. Transferred to 57th (Lowland) Medium Brigade RGA by AO 72/21.

23. North Bucks Cadet Corps, Church Lads Brigade: Rec. 24.11.11 (Bucks) (AO 143/12). Redes **5th Oxford Cadet Corps, CLB** by AO 207/12.

24. Northern Polytechnic School (Holloway) Cadet Corps: Rec. 28.4.16 (County of London) (AO 406/16) and aff. to 19th Bn. London Regt. Inc. to three companies by AO 340/19. Transferred to City of London TFA by AO 255/20. Amal. with Haberdashers (Hampstead) School Cadet Corps and designated **2nd Cadet Bn. Royal Fusiliers (Secondary Schools)** by AO 72/21.

25. North Kent Engineer Cadet Corps: Rec. 22.2.18 (Kent) (AO 173/18) and aff. to Kent (Fortress) RE.

26. North Lancashire Regt.,1st Cadet Battalion: Rec. 28.4.17 (West Lancs) (AO 275/17) and aff. to 4th Bn.

27. North London Cadets: Rec. 12.3.18 (County of London) (AO 173/18). Disbanded by AO 156/20.

28. North Paddington Cadets, 1st: Rec. 17.10.11 (County of London) (AO 347/11). Aff. to 3rd Bn. London Regt. by AO 62/16. Transferred to City of London TFA by AO 262/16. Redes. **3rd Bn. London Regt. Cadet Corps** by AO 406/16.

29. North Riding Volunteer Regt.,2/1st Battalion Cadet Company: Rec. 7.1.18 (North Yorks) (AO 149/18). Disbanded by AO 103/19.

30. North Riding Volunteer Regt.,2nd Battalion Cadet Company: Rec. 13.12.17 (North Yorks) (AO 111/18). Became part of the Cadet Battalion, 5th Bn. Yorkshire Regt. by AO 116/20.

31. North Riding Volunteer Regt.,1/3rd Battalion Cadet Company: Rec. 22.5.18 (North Yorks) (AO 209/18). Disbanded by AO 156/20.

32. North Riding Volunteer Regt.,2/3rd Battalion Cadet Company: Rec. 25.2.18 (North Yorks) (AO 149/18). Inc. to three companies and redes. **"Battalion"** by AO 240/18. Became part of the Cadet Battalion, 4th Bn. Yorkshire Regt. by AO 116/20.

33. North Riding Volunteer Regt.,4th Battalion Cadet Company: Rec. 24.11.17 (North Yorks) (AO 149/18). Disbanded by AO 156/20.

34. North Staffordshire Regt.,1st Volunteer Battalion, 1st Cadet Battalion: Rec. 4.5.18 (Stafford) (AO 373/18). Disbanded by AO 514/20.

35. North Staffordshire Regt.,1st Cadet Battalion: Rec. 25.8.17 (Stafford) (AO 360/17) and aff. to 6th Bn. Absorbed Stafford Cadet Corps by AO 360/17.

36. North Staffordshire Regt.,2nd Cadet Battalion: Rec. 15.3.20 (Stafford) (AO 514/20) and aff. to 5th Bn.

37. Northumberland Fusiliers, 1st, 2nd, 3rd, 5th Cadet Battalions: See Northumberland Volunteer Cadet Brigade.

38. Northumberland Fusiliers, 1st Cadet Brigade: See Northumberland Volunteer Cadet Brigade.

39. Northumberland Volunteer Cadet Brigade: Rec. 3.5.18 (Northumberland) (AO 240/18) and aff. to Northumberland Volunteer Regt. Redes. **1st Cadet Brigade, Northumberland Fusiliers** by AO 373/18. Brigade divided to form **1st, 2nd, 3rd and 5th Cadet Battalions Northumberland Fusiliers** and aff. to 6th Bn. Northumberland Fusiliers (1st CB), Tynemouth RGA (2nd and 3rd CBs), 7th Bn. Northumberland Fusiliers (5th CB) by AO 406/20.

40. Northumbrian Brigade RFA, 2nd, No1 (North Riding) Cadet Battery: Rec. 29.4.15 (North Yorks) (AO 225/15). disbanded by AO 211/20.

41. Northumbrian Brigade RFA, 2nd, No2 (North Riding) Cadet Battery: Rec. 21.12.16 (North Riding) (AO 95/17). Disbanded by AO 211/20.

42. Norton Training School Cadet Corps: Rec. 17.3.17 (Warwick) (AO 168/17) and aff. to 6th Bn. Royal Warwickshire Regt.

43. Norwich Cadet Corps, 1st, Church Lads Brigade: Rec. 11.7.14 (Norfolk) (AO 416/14). Absorbed Melton Constable Cadet Company CLB by AO 360/17.

44. Norwich Cadet Battalion, 2nd, Church Lads Brigade: Rec. 20.11.11 (Suffolk) (AO 41/12). Redes. **1st St. Edmundsbury and Ipswich Bn. CLB** by AO 62/16.

45. Norwich Cadet Battalion, 3rd, Church Lads Brigade: Rec. 23.3.12 (Norfolk) (AO 233/12). Renumbered 2nd by AO 96/16. Reduced to three companies by AO 29/23.

46. Norwich, City of, School Cadet Corps: Rec. 1.3.19 (Norfolk) (AO 137/19) and aff. to 4th Bn. Norfolk Regt.

47. Norwich Grammar School Cadet Corps: Rec. 8.1.16 (Norfolk) (AO 62/16) and aff. to 4th Bn. Norfolk Regt. Disbanded by AO 459/20.

48. Norwich High School Cadets: Rec. 19.10.15 (Norfolk) (AO 62/16) and aff. to 4th Bn. Norfolk Regt. Inc. to two companies by AO 419/19.

49. Nottingham Cadet Battalion, 1st. Rec. 28.8.14 (Nottingham)(AO 416/14). Redes. **1st Nottingham (Church) Cadet Bn.** by AO 511/14. Disbanded by AO 211/20.

50. Nottingham Cadet Battalion, 1st, The Boys Brigade: Rec. 10.4.19 (AO 251/19).

51. Nottingham (Church) Cadet Battalion, 1st: See 1st Nottingham Cadet Bn.

52. Nottinghamshire and Derbyshire Regt.,1st Cadet Battalion: Rec. 25.11.14 (Nottingham) (AO 41/15) and aff. to 7th Bn.

53. Nottinghamshire and Derbyshire Regt.,2nd Cadet Battalion (Magnus Grammar School Cadet Corps): Rec. 14.6.17 (Nottingham) (AO 275/17) and aff. to 8th Bn. Absorbed into Notts Secondary Schools Cadet Bn. 14.3.18 (AO 173/18).

54. Nottinghamshire Secondary Schools Cadet Battalion: Rec. 14.3.18 (Nottingham) (AO 173/18) and aff. to 8th Bn. Notts and Derby Regt. Absorbed 2nd Cadet Bn. Notts and Derby Regt. upon formation. Reduced to three companies by AO 435/22.

55. Nuneaton Cadet Corps: 1.5.19 (Warwick) (AO 219/19) and aff. to 7th Bn. Royal Warwickshire Regt. Inc. to two companies by AO 276/19. Disbanded by AO 452/21.

O

1. Oban High School Cadet Corps: Rec. 17.4.18 (Argyll) (AO 173/18) and aff. to 1st Bn. Argyllshire Volunteer Regt. Transfered to 8th Bn. Argyll and Sutherland Highlanders by AO 116/20.

2. Oldbury Secondary School Cadet Company: Rec. 26.6.15 (Worcs) (AO 302/15) and aff. to 7th Bn. Worcestershire Regt. Became part of Worcestershire Cadet Bn. by AO 188/16.

3. Ongar Grammar School Cadet Corps: Rec. 29.6.10 (Essex) (AO 197/10) and aff. to 4th Bn. Essex Regt. Inc. to three companies by AO 51/18. Reduced to one company by AO 150/22.

4. Oratory Boys Brigade: Rec. 1.3.11 (County of London) (AO 130/11).

5. Orient College (Skegness) Cadet Company: Rec. 18.1.16 (Lincoln) (AO 96/16). Disbanded by AO 514/20.

6. Orsett Cadets: Rec. 21.4.17 (Essex) (AO 275/17) and aff. to 6th Bn. Essex Regt. Disbanded by AO 118/21.

7. Ovingdean School Cadet Corps: Rec. 10.10.21 (Sussex) (AO 527/21) and aff. to 4th Bn. Royal Sussex Regt.

8. Owen's School (Islington) Cadet Corps: Rec. 5.11.14 (County of London) (AO 511/14). disbanded by AO 527/21.

9. Oxford Cadet Battalion, 1st, Church Lads Brigade: Rec. 29.4.12 (Oxford) (AO 207/12).

10. Oxford Cadet Battalion, 2nd, Church Lads Brigade: Rec. 11.5.12 (Berks) (AO 177/12).

11. Oxford Cadet Battalion, 3rd, Church Lads Brigade: Rec. 25.8.11 (Bucks) (AO 347/11).

12. Oxford Cadet Battalion, 4th, Church Lads Brigade: Rec. 9.10.12 (Berks) (AO 320/12).

13. Oxford Cadet Corps, 5th, Church Lads Brigade: See North Bucks Cadet Corps CLB.

14. Oxton, 1st, (Birkenhead School) Cadet Corps: Rec. 22.10.14 (Chester) (AO 511/14) and aff. to 4th Bn. Cheshire Regt. Redes. **Birkenhead School Cadet Corps** by AO 381/15.

P

1. Paddington Boys Club and Naval Brigade: Rec. 2.8.12 (County of London) (AO 235/13). Transferred to the admin. of the Admiralty by AO 116/20.

2. Padstow Cadet Company, Church Lads Brigade: Rec. 28.4.16 (Cornwall) (AO 188/16). AO 229/16 directed that - "the raising of the unit will be held in abeyance during the war". Reinstated by AO 128/17.

3. Paisley Cadet Companies, The Boys Brigade: 1st rec. 5.6.18 (AO 307/18), **2nd** rec. 14.6.18 (AO 307/18), **5th** rec. 16.7.18 (AO 307/18), **7th** rec. 9.5.18 (AO 209/18), **9th** rec. 28.5.18 (AO 307/18), **12th** 27.5.18 (AO 307/18), **13th** rec. 7.3.21 (AO 184/21), **20th** rec. 25.5.18 (AO 307/18), **21st** rec. 7.3.21 (AO 184/21), rec withdrawn by AO 435/22, **22nd** rec. 10.5.18 (AO 209/18). All units admin. by Renfrew TFA.

4. Palmer's School Cadet Corps: Rec. 31.8.10 (Essex) (AO 258/10) and aff. to 6th Bn. Essex Regt. Inc. to three companies by AO 137/19. Inc. to four companies and redes. **10th Cadet Bn. (Palmer's School) Essex Regt.** by AO 419/19.

5. Pannal Ash College Cadet Corps: Rec. 21.7.15 (West Yorks) (AO 343/15) and aff. to 5th Bn. West Yorkshire Regt.

6. Parmiter's School Cadet Corps: Rec. 4.5.15 (City of London) (AO 225/15) and aff. to 5th Bn. London Regt. Amal. with Coopers' Company's School to form **2nd City of London Cadet Bn. (Secondary Schools)** by AO 229/16.

7. Paston School Cadet Corps: Rec. 14.9.18 (Norfolk) (AO 342/18) and aff. to 5th Bn. Norfolk Regt. Inc. to three companies by AO 419/19.

8. Patricroft Parish Cadet Company, Church Lads Brigade: Rec. 1.11.12 (East Lancs) (AO 343/12). Absorbed into 5th Manchester Cadet Bn. CLB by AO 457/15.

9. Pearson and Knowles Cadet Corps: Rec. 8.7.21 (West Lancs) (AO 365/21) and aff. to 4th Bn. South Lancashire Regt.

10. Penrith Cadet Company: Rec. 23.9.17 (Cumberland) (AO 360/17) and aff. to 1/1st Bn. Cumberland Volunteer Regt. Aff. transferred to 4th Bn. Border Regt. by AO 116/20. Disbanded by AO 72/21.

11. Pershore and Cropthorne Cadet Company: Rec. 20.10.17 (Worcs) (AO 51/18) and aff. to 2nd Bn. Worcestershire Volunteer Regt. Transferred to 8th Bn. Worcester Regt. by AO 116/20.

12. Perth Academy Cadet Corps: Rec. 28.9.17 (Perth) (AO 360/17).

13. Perth, City of, Cadet Corps: Rec. 15.11.18 (Perth) (AO 31/19). Disbanded by AO 24/20.

14. Perthshire Cadet Battalion, 1st, The Boys Brigade: Rec. 28.9.17 (Perth) (AO 360/17). Inc. to five companies by AO 24/20. Inc. to six companies by AO 25/21.

15. Peterborough Cadet Battalion, 1st, Church Lads Brigade: Rec. 15.11.12 (Leicester) (AO 343/12).

16. Peterborough Cadet Battalion, 3rd, Church Lads Brigade: Rec. 28.6.12 (Northampton) (AO 233/12). Inc. to twelve companies by AO 219/19. Redes.   **3rd Peterborough (Northampton)** by AO 493/21.

17. Peterborough Cadet Battalion, 4th, Church Lads Brigade: Rec. 17.11.15 (Leicester) (AO 23/16).

18. Peter Symonds School Cadet Corps: Rec. 9.7.13 (Southampton) (AO 274/13) and aff. to 4th Bn. Hampshire Regt. Amal. with 1st Cadet Bn. Hampshire Regt. and Aldershot County School to form **1/4th and 2/4th Hampshire Regt. Cadet Bn.** by AO 307/18.

19. Plymouth Boys Brigade: See Boys Brigade Cadet Bn. Plymouth.

20. Plymouth Cadet Corps: See Plymouth Lads Brigade.

21. Plymouth Lads Brigade Cadet Corps: Rec. 14.12.10 (Devon) (AO 40/11) and aff. to 5th Bn. Devonshire Regt. Inc. to three companies by AO 360/17. Redes. **Plymouth Cadet Corps** by AO 452/21.

22. Pocklington School Cadet Corps: Rec. 3.5.16 (East Yorks) (AO 188/16). Aff. to 4th Bn. East Yorkshire Regt. by AO 255/20.

23. Polytechnic Schools Cadet Corps: Rec. 18.12.14 (County of London) (AO 79/15) and aff. to 12th Bn. London Regt. Reduced to five companies by AO 310/22.

24. Portsmouth Division, Royal Marine Light Infantry Cadets: Rec. 7.7.19 (Southampton) (AO 419/19).

25. Port Sunlight Cadet Company, 1st, The Boys Brigade: Rec. 4.1.18 (Chester) (AO 149/18).

26. Port Talbot County School Cadet Corps: Rec. 21.4.17 (Glamorgan) (AO 275/17) and aff. to 7th Bn. Welsh Regt. Disbanded by AO 156/20.

27. Poulton Cadet Company, 1st: Rec. 24.9.13 (Chester) (AO 373/13) and aff. to 4th Bn. Cheshire Regt. Disbanded by AO 381/19.

28. Prestonpans Cadet Corps: Rec. 12.2.13 (Haddington) (AO 86/13) and aff. to 8th Bn. Royal Scots.

29. Princetown Cadet Company, Church Lads Brigade: Rec. 30.9.11 (Devon) (AO 41/12). Disbanded by AO 25/21.

30. Purley County School Cadet Corps: Rec. 15.11.15 (Surrey) (AO 457/15) and aff. to 4th Bn. Royal West Surrey Regt. Became part of 3rd Cadet Bn. Royal West Surrey Regt. by AO 103/19.

31. Putney Cadet Corps: Rec. 13.3.22 (County of London) (AO 265/22).

32. Pwllheli County School Cadet Corps: Rec. 23.3.17 (Carnarvon) (AO 168/17). Disbanded by AO 323/21.

Q

1. Queen Elizabeth Grammar School Cadet Corps: Rec. 11.3.18 (Westmoreland) (AO 173/18) and aff. to 2nd Cumberland and Westmoreland Volunteer Bn. The Border Regt. Transfered to 4th Bn. Border Regt. by AO 116/20.

2. Queen Elizabeth's, Ashbourne Cadet Corps: Rec. 4.2.17 (Derby) (AO 149/18) and aff. to 5th Derbyshire Volunteer Regt. Absorbed into the Derbyshire Schools Cadet Bn. by AO 219/19.

3. Queen Elizabeth's School, Barnet: See 7th Hertfordshire Cadets.

4. Queen's College (Taunton) Cadet Battalion: Rec. 7.5.15 (Somerset) (AO 225/15). Aff. to 5th Bn. Somerset Light Infantry by AO 381/15.

5. Queen's Westminster Cadet Corps: Rec. 5.12.10 (County of London) (AO 161/11) and aff. to 16th Bn. London Regt. Reduced to two companies by AO 310/22.

6. Queen's Westminster Cadet Corps, 3rd: Rec. 13.10.17 (County of London) (AO 51/18) and aff. to 16th Bn. London Regt. Rec. withdrawn by AO 29/23.

R

1. Raine's School (Stepney) Cadet Corps: Rec. 6.10.16 (County of London) (AO 24/17) and aff. to 17th Bn. London Regt. Amal. with George Green's School Cadet Corps to form **3rd City of London Cadet Bn.** by AO 275/17.

2. Ramsey Grammar School Cadet Corps: Rec. 16.1.18 (Hunts) (AO 149/18). Disbanded by AO 493/21.

3. Ramsgate County School Cadet Corps: Rec. 8.10.15 (Kent) (AO 430/15) and aff. to 4th Bn. East Kent Regt. Absorbed into Kent Public Secondary Schools Cadet Bn. by AO 137/19.

4. Readheads Cadet Corps: Rec. 9.11.18 (Durham) (AO 69/19) and aff. to 7th Bn. Durham Light Infantry.

5. Reading Cadet Battalion: The battalion was aff. to 4th Bn. Royal Berkshire Regt. and admin. by the Berks TFA. Its companies were formed as follows:- **Sutton's Company:** Rec. 10.6.18 (AO 240/18). Disbanded by AO 459/20. **No2 (Town) Company:** Rec. 17.6.18 (AO 240/18). Redes. **(The Brigade) Company** by AO 459/20 **Herbert's Company:** Rec. 20.6.18 (AO 240/18). **Huntley and Palmers Company:** Rec.

27.6.18 (AO 240/18). Disbandment ordered by AO 118/21 but cancelled by AO 184/21. **No5 (Pulsometer) Engineer Company:** Rec. 1.7.18 (AO 307/18). Disbanded by AO 459/20. **No6 (Warricks & Allen & Simmonds) Company:** Rec. 1.8.18 (AO 307/18). Disbanded by AO 459/20. **No7 (Huntley & Palmers) Company:** Rec. 13.5.19 (AO 251/19). Disbandment ordered by AO 118/21 but cancelled by AO 184/21. **No8 (St. Andrew's Home) Company:** See Reading Cadet Company.

6. Reading Cadet Company: Rec. 13.11.15 (Berks) (AO 457/15) and aff. to 4th Bn. Royal Berkshire Regt. Redes. **No8 (St. Andrew's Home) Company, Reading Cadet Bn.** by AO 373/18.

7. Reading Cadet Company, 7th, The Boys Brigade: Rec. 1.5.22 (Berks) (AO 265/22).

8. Redditch Cadet Company: Rec. 20.7.18 (Worcs) (AO 342/18) and aff. to 3rd Volunteer Bn. Worcestershire Regt. Disbanded by AO 116/20.

9. Redhill and Nutfield Company, 7th Southwark Cadet Battalion, Church Lads Brigade: Rec. 11.12.11 (Surrey) (AO 11/12).

10. Reigate Cadet Company, 1st, The Boys Brigade: Rec. 8.11.18 (Surrey) (AO 31/19). Became part of 1st Surrey Cadet Bn. The Boys Brigade by AO 61/20.

11. Reigate Cadet Company, 2nd, The Boys Brigade: Rec. 21.10.18 (Surrey) (AO 31/19). Became part of 1st Surrey Cadet Bn. The Boys Brigade by AO 61/20.

12. Reigate Company, 7th Southwark Cadet Battalion, Church Lads Brigade: Rec. 11.12.11 (Surrey) (AO 11/12).

13. Renfrewshire Volunteer Regt., 1st Cadet Company, 1/1st Battalion: Rec. 15.2.18 (Renfrew) (AO 209/18). Transfered and redes. **1st Cadet Company, 5th Bn. Argyll and Sutherland Highlanders** by AO 116/20, now aff. to 6th Bn.

14. Rhyl County School Cadet Corps: Rec. 22.6.16 (Flint) (AO 302/16) and aff. to 5th Bn. Royal Welsh Fusiliers. Became part of 1st Cadet Bn. 5th Bn. Royal Welsh Fusiliers by AO 240/18.

15. Richmond Boys Naval Cadets: Rec. 3.12.17 (Surrey) (AO 111/18) and aff. to 8th Bn. Surrey Volunteer Regt. Amal. with Wimbledon Naval Brigade to form **2nd Cadet Bn. East Surrey Regt.** by AO 103/19.

16. Richmond County School Cadet Corps: Rec. 10.10.10 (Surrey) (AO 281/10) and aff. to 6th Bn. East Surrey Regt. Became part of 1st Cadet Bn. East Surrey Regt by AO 103/19.

17. Richmond Hill Cadets: Rec. 9.11.14 (Surrey) (AO 511/14) and aff. to 6th Bn. East Surrey Regt. Absorbed into 1st Cadet Bn. East Surrey Regt. by AO 103/19.

18. Rich School Cadet Corps: Rec. 19.3.17 (Gloucester) (AO 168/17) and aff. to 5th Bn. Gloucestershire Regt.

19. Ripon Cadet Battalion, 1st, Church Lads Brigade: Rec. 1.1.12 (West Yorks) (AO 41/12).

20. Ripon Cadet Battalion, 2nd, Church Lads Brigade: Rec. 1.1.12 (West Yorks) (AO 41/12). Absorbed St. John's Bailson Cadet Company, CLB by AO 149/18. Redes. **1st Bradford Cadet Bn. CLB** by AO 116/20.

21. Ripon Cadet Corps, 3rd, Church Lads Brigade: Rec. 1.1.14 (West Yorks) (AO 38/14). Redes. **2nd Ripon Cadet Bn. CLB** by AO 116/20.

22. Ripon School Cadet Corps: Rec. 7.12.15 (West Yorks) (AO 23/16) and aff. to 5th Bn. West Yorkshire Regt.

23. Risca and Cross Keys Cadet Corps: See 1st Cadet Bn. Monmouthshire Regt.

24. Rishworth Grammar School Cadet Corps: Rec. 2.11.21 (West Yorks) (AO 265/22) and aff. to 4th Bn. Duke of Wellington's Regt.

25. Roan School (Greenwich) Cadet Corps: Rec. 10.7.15 (County of London) (AO 302/15) and aff. to 20th Bn. London Regt. Disbanded by AO 493/21.

26. Roborough School (Eastbourne) Cadet Company: Rec. 9.11.14 (Sussex) (AO 225/15) and aff. to 2nd Home Counties Brigade RFA. Redes. as "Corps" by AO 457/15.

27. Rochester Cadet Battalion, Church Lads Brigade: Rec. 13.9.11 (Kent) (AO 233/12).

28. Romford Company, 1st, The Boys Brigade Cadets: Rec. 21.5.18 (Essex) (AO 240/18).

29. Romford Company, 2nd, The Boys Brigade Cadets: Rec. 30.4.19 (Essex) (AO 251/19). Disbanded by AO 483/22.

30. Row Company, 1st, The Boys Brigade Cadets: Rec. 5.9.17 (Dumbarton) (AO 360/17).

31. Royal Masonic School Cadets (11th Hertfordshire): Rec. 28.9.17 (Hertford) (AO 111/18) and aff. to 5th Bn. London Regt.

32. Ruabon Grammar School Cadet Corps: Rec. 30.7.17 (Denbigh) (AO 360/17) and aff. to 4th Bn. Royal Welsh Fusiliers. Inc. to two companies by AO 483/22.

33. Rugeley Grammar School Cadet Corps: Rec. 25.9.15 (Stafford) (AO 430/15) and aff. to 6th Bn. North Staffordshire Regt. Absorbed into 1st Cadet Bn. Secondary Schools (Staffordshire Regt.) by AO 373/18.

34. Russell Hill Cadet Corps (Warehousemen, Clerks and Drapers' Schools): Rec. 9.10.16 (Surrey) (AO 375/16). Aff. to 4th Bn. Royal West Surrey Regt. by AO 360/17. Became part of 3rd Cadet Bn. Royal West Surrey Regt. by AO 103/19.

35. Ruthin School Cadet Corps: Rec. 12.3.14 (Denbigh) (AO 188/14). Aff. to 4th Bn. Royal Welsh Fusiliers by AO 275/17.

36. Rutland Regt.,1st Cadet Battalion: Rec. 16.11.17 (Leicester) (AO 111/18) and aff. to 5th Bn. Leicestershire Regt. Disbanded by AO 116/20.

37. Rutland Street (LCC) School Cadet Corps: Rec. 21.3.11 (City of London) (AO 161/11). Aff. to 10th Bn. London Regt. by AO 139/15. Redes. **Tower Hamlets Cadets (10th Cadets, City of London)** by AO 261/15. Absorbed Marner School Cadet Corps by AO 188/16.

38. Rutlish School Cadet Corps: Rec. 21.3.21 (Surrey) (AO 184/21) and aff. to 5th Bn. East Surrey Regt.

39. Rydal Mount School (Colwyn Bay) Cadet Corps: Rec. 24.10.16 (Denbigh) (AO 406/16) and aff. to 4th Bn. Royal Welsh Fusiliers.

40. Ryde Cadet Company: Rec. 17.8.15 (Southampton) (AO 430/15) and aff. to 8th Bn. Hampshire Regt. Absorbed into 3rd Cadet (Isle of Wight) Bn. The Hampshire Regt. by AO 457/15. Removed from battalion by AO 25/21, redes. **1st (Ryde) Cadet Company** and aff. to 55th (Wessex) Brigade RFA.

41. Rylands Bros. (Warrington) Cadet Corps: Rec. 24.3.19 (West Lancs) (AO 219/19) and aff. to 4th Bn. South Lancashire Regt.

S

1. St. Aidan's, Carlisle Cadet Company, Church Lads Brigade: Rec. 11.6.18 (Cumberland) (AO 240/18).

2. St. Albans Battalion, 1st, Church Lads Brigade: Rec. 20.9.11 (Essex) (AO 316/11). Redes. **1st Chelmsford Cadet Bn. CLB** by AO 63/14. Inc. to twelve companies by AO 406/20.

3. St. Albans Battalion, 2nd, Church Lads Brigade: Rec. 10.5.12 (Hertford) (AO 177/12). Renumbered **1st** by AO 104/14. Reduced to three companies by AO 95/22.

4. St. Albans Battalion, 3rd, Church Lads Brigade: Rec. 10.5.12 (Hertford) (AO 177/12). Renumbered **2nd** by AO 104/14. See also 1st Bn. Ely Regt. CLB

5. St. Albans Battalion, 4th, Church Lads Brigade: Rec. 13.9.11 (Essex) (AO 347/11). Redes. **2nd Chelmsford Cadet Bn. CLB** by AO 63/14. Reduced to four companies by AO 150/22.

6. St. Albans Battalion, 5th, Church Lads Brigade: Rec. 31.10.11 (Essex) (AO 347/11). Redes. **3rd Chelmsford Cadet Bn. CLB** by AO 63/14. Inc. to five companies by AO 31/19. Reduced to two companies by AO 150/22.

7. St. Andrew's, Chesterton Cadet Company, Church Lads Brigade: Rec. 6.5.22 (Cambs and Ely) (AO 265/22).

8. St. Andrew's (West Kensington) Cadet Corps: Rec. 5.1.16 (County of London) (AO 96/16) and aff. to 14th Bn. London Regt. Disbanded by AO 452/21.

9. St. Anne's (Blackburn) Cadet Company Salford Diocesan Catholic Boys Brigade: Rec. 6.6.19 (East Lancs) (AO 276/19). Disbanded by AO 514/20.

10. St. Anne's, Lancaster Cadet Company, Church Lads Brigade: Rec. 18.1.15 (West Lancs) (AO 225/15). Disbanded 5.1.17 (AO 149/18).

11. St. Anne's-on-Sea Cadet Company, Church Lads Brigade: Rec. 12.6.18 (West Lancs) (AO 240/18).

12. St. Anne's School Cadet Corps: Rec. 10.4.11 (City of London) (AO 161/11). Absorbed into 1st Cadet Bn. King's Royal Rifle Corps by AO 275/17.

13. St. Asaph Cadet Battalion, 1st, Church Lads Brigade: Rec. 17.10.13 (Flint) (AO 398/13).

14. St. Asaph School Cadet Corps: Rec. 22.6.16 (Flint) (AO 302/16) and aff. to 5th Bn. Royal Welsh Fusiliers. Became part of 1st Cadet Bn. 5th Bn. Royal Welsh Fusiliers by AO 240/18.

15. **St. Augustine's College (Ramsgate) Cadet Corps:** Rec. 25.2.16 (Kent) (AO 160/16) and aff. to 4th Bn. East Kent Regt. Placed into abeyance by AO 360/17.

16. **St. Austin's Company, Catholic Boys Brigade:** Rec. 22.4.14 (West Yorks) (AO 188/14). Redes. **St. Austin's (Wakefield)** Company by AO 257/14.

17. **St. Barabas, Anne and John's Derby Cadet Company, Church Lads Brigade:** Rec. 23.7.18 (Derby) (AO 307/18). Absorbed into 5th Southwell Cadet Bn. CLB by AO 31/19.

18. **St. Barabas, Hove Cadet Company, Church Lads Brigade:** Rec. 21.3.21 (Sussex) (AO 452/21).

19. **St. Barnabas, Morecambe Cadet Company, Church Lads Brigade:** Rec. 26.2.15 (West Lancs) (AO 225/15). Rec. withdrawn by AO 317/20.

20. **St. Bartholomew's, Porthleven Cadet Company, Church Lads Brigade:** Rec. 28.4.16 (Cornwall) (AO 188/16). Disbanded by AO 493/21.

21. **St. Christopher's Cadet Corps:** Rec. 10.11.14 (City of London) (AO 79/15). Inc. to four companies by AO 173/18. Became part of 1st Cadet Bn. 4th Bn. London Regt. by AO 156/20.

22. **St. Cross, Knutsford Cadet Company, Church Lads Brigade:** Rec. 7.9.11 (Chester) (AO 284/11). Rec. withdrawn by AO 61/20.

23. **St. Cuthbert's Grammar School Cadet Unit:** Rec. 3.8.17 (Northumberland) (AO 51/18) and aff. to 6th Bn. Northumberland Fusiliers. Rec. withdrawn by AO 355/22.

24. **St. Cyprian's Kirkmanhulme Cadet Company, Church Lads Brigade:** Rec. 17.3.16 (East Lancs) (AO 125/16). Absorbed into 2nd Manchester Cadet Bn. CLB by AO 275/17.

25. **St. David's Cadet Battalion, 1st, Church Lads Brigade:** Rec. 6.7.12 (Glamorgan) (AO 233/12).

26. **St. David's Cadet Battalion, 2nd, Church Lads Brigade:** Rec. 1.1.18 (Carmarthen) (AO 149/18). Absorbed Holy Trinity, Aberystwyth Cadet Company CLB by AO 493/21.

27. **St. David's Cadet Company, Church Lads Brigade:** Rec. 15.7.14 (Carmarthen) (AO 261/15). Redes. **St. David's, Carmarthen Cadet Company CLB** by AO 381/15.

28. **St. David's, Carmarthen Cadet Company, Church Lads Brigade:** See St. David's Cadet Company CLB.

29. **St. Dunstan's College Cadet Corps:** Rec. 10.3.11 (County of London) (AO 161/11) and aff. to 20th Bn. London Regt. Transfered to the OTC by AO 284/11.

30. **St. Edmund's College Company:** See 8th Hertfordshire Cadets.

31. **St. Edmundsbury and Ipswich Battalion, 1st, Church Lads Brigade:** See 2nd Norwich Cadet Bn. CLB.

32. **St. Gabriel's, Canning Town Cadet Company ("C" Company, 1st Cadet Bn. Essex Regt.):** Rec. 15.6.10 (Essex) (AO 197/10) and aff. to 6th Bn. Essex Regt. Became part of 1st Cadet Bn. by AO 65/11.

33. **St. George's Secondary School Cadet Corps:** Rec. 18.6.17 (Gloucester) (AO 275/17) and aff. to 4th Bn. Gloucestershire Regt. Disbanded by AO 419/19.

34. **St. George's Cadet Corps, Eastbourne:** Rec. 16.11.16 (Sussex) (AO 128/17) and aff. to 1st Home Counties Field Company, RE. Disbanded 15.4.17 (AO 111/18).

35. **St. George's College Cadets:** See 3rd Cadet Company, 6th Bn. East Surrey Regt.

36. **St. George's School Company:** See 4th Hertfordshire Cadets.

37. **St. Gerard's (Lostock Hall) Cadet Company, Salford Diocesan Catholic Boys Brigade:** Rec. 16.6.19 (West Lancs) (AO 276/19).

38. **St. Gilbert's Cadet Company, Winton, Salford Diocesan Catholic Boys Brigade:** Rec. 9.5.19 (East Lancs) (AO 251/19). Absorbed into 7th Cadet Bn. Salford Diocesan Catholic Boys Brigade by AO 340/19.

39. **St. Gwlady's, Bargoed Company, Church Lads Brigade:** Rec. 15.8.11 (Glamorgan) (AO 284/11). Absorbed into 3rd Llandaff Cadet Bn, CLB by AO 144/14.

40. **St. Hugh's (Bickley) Cadet Corps:** Rec. 1.5.18 (Kent) (AO 209/18). Aff. to 5th Bn. Royal West Kent Regt. by AO 493/21. Disbanded by AO 483/22.

41. **St. James's, Whitehaven Cadet Corps, Church Lads Brigade:** Rec. 6.4.16 (Cumberland) (AO 160/16). Disbanded by AO 72/21.

42. **St. John's and St. Peter's, Plymouth Cadet Company, Church Lads Brigade:** See St. John's, Plymouth.

43. **St. John's, Baildon Cadet Company, Church Lads Brigade:** Rec. 8.2.15 (West Yorks) (AO 109/15). Absorbed into 2nd Ripon Cadet Bn. CLB by AO 149/18.

44. **St. John's Company, Chichester Regiment, Church Lads Brigade:** Rec. 14.1.18 (Sussex) (AO 149/18). Redes. **St. John's Mead's , Eastbourne Cadet Company CLB** by AO 251/19. Disbanded by AO 156/20.

45. **St. John's Mead's, Eastbourne Cadet Company, Church Lads Brigade:** See St. John's Company, Chichester Regt.

46. **St. John's, Peterborough Cadet Company, Church Lads Brigade:** Rec. 27.4.16 (Northampton) (AO 188/16).

47. **St. John's, Plymouth Cadet Corps:** Rec. 3.11.14 (Devon) (AO 41/15). Redes. **St. John's and St. Peter's, Plymouth Cadet Company, CLB** by AO 109/15. Disbanded by AO 25/21.

48. **St. Joseph's College (Dumfries) Cadet Corps:** Rec. 2.3.15 (Dumfries) (AO 139/15) and aff. to 5th Bn. King's Own Scottish Borderers.

49. **St. Leonard's Collegiate School Cadet Company:** See Collegiate School Cadet Company, Hastings.

50. **St. Luke's and Linton Cadet Corps, Church Lads Brigade:** See St. Luke's, Cambridge.

51. **St. Luke's, Cambridge Cadet Company, Church Lads Brigade:** Rec. 8.7.16 (Cambs and Ely) (AO 262/16). Inc. to two companies and redes. **St. Luke's and Linton Cadet Corps, CLB** by AO 323/21.

52. **St. Margaret, Whalley Range and St. Clement's, Urmston Cadet Corps, Church Lads Brigade:** Rec. 4.12.14 (East Lancs) (AO 79/15). Redes. **6th Manchester Cadet Bn. CLB** by AO 343/15. Inc. to eight companies by AO 219/19. Reduced to six companies by AO 435/22. Reduced to two companies by AO 483/22.

53. **St. Mark's (Peckham) Cadet Corps:** Rec. 22.5.14 (County of London) (AO 343/15). Inc. to two companies by AO 340/19. Disbanded by AO 95/22.

54. **St. Mark's, West Gorton Cadet Company, Church Lads Brigade:** Rec. 15.3.15 (East Lancs) (AO 381/15). Absorbed into 2nd Manchester Cadet Bn. CLB by AO 275/17.

55. **St. Mary's (Brownedge) Cadet Company, Salford Diocesan Catholic Boys Brigade:** Rec. 16.6.19 (West Lancs) (AO 276/19).

56. **St. Mary's Builth Wells Cadet Company, Church Lads Brigade:** Rec. 13.11.14 (Brecknock) (AO 511/14). Disbanded by AO 265/22.

57. **St. Mary's (St. Helens) Cadet Company, Church Lads Brigade:** Rec. 7.10.21 (West Lancs) (AO 452/21).

58. **St. Mary's (Swinton) Cadet Company, Salford Diocesan Catholic Boys Brigade:** Rec. 6.6.19 (East Lancs) (AO 276/19). Absorbed into 7th Cadet Bn. Salford Diocesan Catholic Boys Brigade by AO 340/19.

59. **St. Mary's, Walney Island Cadet Company, Church Lads Brigade:** Rec. 24.3.16 (West Lancs) (AO 160/16). Rec. withdrawn by AO 317/20.

60. **St. Matthew's (Custom House) Cadet Company ("D" Company, 1st Cadet Bn. Essex Regt.):** Rec. 25.1.11 (Essex) (AO 65/11). Became part of 1st Cadet Bn. Essex Regt. by AO 65/11.

61. **St. Matthew's (Preston) Cadet Company, Church Lads Brigade:** Rec. 16.3.18 (West Lancs) (AO 149/18). Absorbed into 11th Manchester Cadet Bn. CLB by AO 72/21.

62. **St. Michael's, Aberystwyth Cadet Company, Church Lads Brigade:** Rec. 1.6.16 (Cardigan) (AO 229/16). Disbanded 31.5.18 (AO 342/18).

63. **St. Michael's School Company:** See 15th Hertfordshire Cadets.

64. **St. Nicholas Company:** See 1st Lincoln Cadet Bn. CLB.

65. **St. Ninian's Company, 1st, Boys Brigade Cadets:** Rec. 2.5.22 (Stirling) (AO 265/22).

66. **St. Olave's School Cadet Corps** 3.12.14 (County of London) (AO 79/15) and aff. to 21st Bn. London Regt. Redes. **St. Olave's and St. Saviour's School Cadet Corps** by AO 261/15.

67. **St. Pancras Cadet Corps:** Rec. 17.12.17 (County of London) (AO 111/18) and aff. to 1/8th Bn. London Volunteer Regt. Transferred to 19th Bn. London Regt. by AO 342/18. Redes. **19th Bn. London Regt. Cadet Corps** by AO 184/21. Reduced to three companies by AO 310/22.

68. **St. Patrick's (Leeds) Company, Catholic Boys Brigade:** Rec. 18.2.14 (West Yorks) (AO 257/14). Disbanded 12.7.16 (AO 128/17).

69. **St. Paul's, Cheltenham Cadet Corps:** Rec. 18.12.17 (Gloucester) (AO 149/18) and aff. to 3rd Bn. Gloucestershire Volunteer Regt.

70. **St. Paul's, Derby Cadet Company, Church Lads Brigade:** Rec. 12.8.18 (Derby) (AO 307/18). Absorbed into 5th Southwell Cadet Bn. CLB by AO 31/19.

71. St. Paul's (Farrington) Cadet Company, Church Lads Brigade: Rec. 29.8.19 (West Lancs) (AO 340/19). Absorbed into 11th Manchester Cadet Bn. CLB by AO 72/21.

72. St. Paul's, Goole Cadet Company, Church Lads Brigade: Rec. 30.6.21 (West Yorks) (AO 323/21).

73. St. Paul's, Llanelly Cadet Corps, Church Lads Brigade: Rec. 30.6.16 (Carmarthen) (AO 262/16).

74. St. Paul's (Longridge) Cadet Company, Church Lads Brigade: Rec. 22.10.20 (West Lancs) (AO 514/20). Absorbed into 11th Manchester Cadet Bn. CLB by AO 72/21.

75. St. Peter and St. Margaret (Fleetwood) Cadet Company, Church Lads Brigade: Rec. 20.4.15 (West Lancs) (AO 23/16).

76. St. Peter's Cadet Company: Rec. 12.3.12 (County of London) (AO 177/12) and aff. to 13th Bn. London Regt. Disbanded by AO 219/19.

77. St. Peter's, Glasgow Company, 2nd Scottish Cadet Battalion, Church Lads Brigade: Rec. 25.3.13 (City of London) (AO 337/13). Redes. "C" Company by AO 218/14. Rec. withdrawn by AO 251/19.

78. St. Peter's (Plymouth) Cadet Company, Church Lads Brigade: Rec. 3.8.15 (Devon) (AO 343/15). Disbanded by AO 156/20.

79. St. Petroc's, Bodmin Cadet Company, Church Lads Brigade: Rec. 28.4.16 (Cornwall) (AO 188/16). Put into temporary abeyance by AO 360/17. Disbanded by AO 514/20.

80. St. Philip's, Arundel Cadet Corps: Rec. 8.7.12 (Sussex) (AO 233/12). Disbanded 5.1.15 (AO 225/15).

81. St. Philip's Grammar School (Edgbaston) Cadet Corps: Rec. 5.2.15 (Warwick) (AO 109/15). Absorbed into 3rd Cadet Bn. Royal Warwickshire Regt. by AO 261/15.

82. St. Thomas (St. Helens) Cadet Company, Church Lads Brigade: Rec. 7.10.21 (West Lancs) (AO 452/21).

83. St. Thomas's (Wandsworth) Cadet Corps: Rec. 26.3.14 (City of London) (AO 144/14) and aff. to 23rd Bn. London Regt. Redes. **Wandsworth Cadet Company (St. Thomas's)** by AO 160/16. Redes. **South West London Cadet Battalion** by AO 95/17. Inc. to eight companies by AO 275/17. Became part of 1st Cadet Bn. 4th Bn. London Regt. by AO 156/20.

84. St. William's School Cadet Corps: Rec. 21.2.19 (East Yorks) (AO 219/19) and aff. to 4th Bn. East Yorkshire Regt.

85. Salford Diocesan Catholic Boys Brigade Cadet Battalions: 1st rec. 14.2.19 (AO 219/19). Inc. to eight companies by AO 61/20. Reduced to seven companies by AO 527/21. Inc. to eight companies by AO 483/22. 2nd rec. 14.2.19 (AO 219/19). Inc. to seven companies by AO 251/19. Reduced to six companies by AO 527/21. 3rd rec. 14.2.19 (AO 219/19). Reduced to three companies by AO 527/21. 4th rec. 14.2.19 (AO 219/19). Reduced to two companies by AO 527/21. 5th rec. 14.2.19 (AO 219/19). Disbanded by AO 514/20. 7th rec. 29.8.19 (AO 340/19). Absorbed All Souls (Weaste), St. Gilbert's (Winton) and St. Mary's (Swinton) Cadet Companies by AO 340/19. All units admin. by East Lancs TFA.

86. Salford Lads Club Cadet Corps: Rec. 27.10.16 (East Lancs) (AO 406/16). Disbanded by AO 381/19.

87. Salisbury (Wiltshire) Cadet Battalion, 1st, Church Lads Brigade: See 3rd Salisbury Cadet Corps CLB.

88. Salisbury Cadet Battalion, 2nd, Church Lads Brigade: Rec. 20.11.11 (Dorset) (AO 11/12). Inc. to eight companies by AO 24/20.

89. Salisbury Cadet Corps, 3rd, Church Lads Brigade: Rec. 22.4.12 (Wilts) (AO 207/12). Amal. with Salisbury Company CLB, inc. to five companies and redes. **1st Salisbury (Wiltshire) Cadet Bn. CLB.** by AO 340/19.

90. Salisbury Company, Salisbury Regiment, Church Lads Brigade: See S.S. Martin and Edmund Cadet Company.

91. Sandbach School Cadet Corps: Rec. 3.1.18 (Chester) (AO 149/18) and aff. to 4th Bn. Cheshire Volunteer Regt. Transfered to 7th Bn. Cheshire Regt. by AO 116/20. Disbanded by AO 527/21.

92. Sandroyd School Troop of Scouts: Rec. 19.6.11 (Surrey) (AO 220/11).

93. Scarborough Municipal School Cadet Corps: Rec. 28.1.15 (North Yorks) (AO 139/15) and aff. to 5th Bn. Yorkshire Regt. Became part of the Cadet Bn. 5th Yorkshire Regt. by AO 116/20. Disbanded by AO 401/22.

94. Scorton Grammar School Cadet Corps: Rec. 25.1.17 (North Yorks) (AO 95/17) and aff. to 4th Bn. Yorkshire Regt. Became part of the Cadet Bn. 4th Yorkshire Regt. by AO 116/20.

95. Scots, Royal, 1st (Edinburgh) Cadet Battalion: See 1st Cadet Bn. City of Edinburgh Volunteer Regt.

96. Scots, Royal, 1st (Highland) Cadet Battalion: Rec. 1.11.11 (City of Edinburgh) (AO 75/12). Aff. to 9th Bn. by AO 24/17.

97. Scots, Royal, 1st Territorial Cadet Battalion: See 1st Cadet Bn. City of Edinburgh Volunteer Regt.

98. Scots Fusiliers, Royal, 1st Cadet Battalion: Rec. 1.11.11 (Ayr) (AO 11/12) and aff. to 4th and 5th Bns. Inc. to eight companies by AO 406/20. Inc. to nine companies by AO 29/23. See also Ayrshire Dockyard Company.

99. Scottish Cadet Battalion, 1st, Church Lads Brigade: Rec. 7.11.11. (City of Edinburgh) (AO 109/12).

100. Scottish Cadet Battalion, 2nd, Church Lads Brigade: Rec. 16.8.12 (Lanark) (AO 13/13). Reduced to one company by AO 493/21.

101. Scottish Engineers Cadet Training Corps: Rec. 11.3.15 (County of London) (AO 225/15). Disbanded by AO 514/20.

102. Seaford College Cadets: Rec. 9.1.11 (Sussex) (AO 130/11).

103. Secondary Schools (Staffordshire Regt.), 1st Cadet Battalion: Rec. 17.6.18 (Stafford) (AO 373/18) and formed by the amal. of Stafford Grammar School, West Bromwich Municiple Secondary School, Tamworth Grammar School, Rugeley Grammar School and Burton-on-Trent Grammar School cadet units.

104. Selby Cadet Company: Rec. 20.9.18 (West Yorks) (AO 342/18) and aff. to 2nd Volunteer Bn. Yorkshire Light Infantry. Disbanded by AO 156/20.

105. Senior Cadet Battalion, 3rd, "A" (Westminster) Company: Rec. 9.1.12 (City of London) (AO 75/12). Disbanded by AO 116/20.

106. Settle Cadet Battalion: Rec. 1.4.10 (West Yorks) (AO 258/10) and aff. to 6th Bn. Duke of Wellington's Regt. Redes. **6th Duke of Wellington's (West Riding) Cadet Bn.** by AO 457/15.

107. Sevenoaks Cadet Company: Rec. 18.6.18 (Kent) (AO 307/18) and aff. to 1st Volunteer Bn. Royal West Kent Regt. Transfered to 4th Bn. by AO 116/20.

108. Severn Cadet Corps: Rec. 10.7.16 (Somerset) (AO 262/16).

109. "Sexeys" School (Blackford) Cadet Corps: See Wedmore Cadet Corps.

110. Shaftesbury Grammar School Cadet Corps: Rec. 20.5.15 (Dorset) (AO 225/15) and aff. to 4th Bn. Dorset Regt.

111. Shanklin Cadet Company: Rec. 28.9.15 (Southampton) (AO 430/15) and aff. to 8th Bn. Hampshire Regt. Absorbed into 3rd Cadet (Isle of Wight) Bn. Hampshire Regt. by AO 457/15.

112. Sheffield Cadet Battalion, The Boys Brigade: Rec. 1.2.21 (West Yorks) (AO 72/21).

113. Sheffield Cadet Battalion, 1st and 2nd, Church Lads Brigade: See 4th and 5th York Cadet Bns. CLB.

114. Shepton Mallet Cadet Corps: Rec. 19.12.17 (Somerset) (AO 111/18) and aff. to 3rd Bn. Somerset Volunteer Regt. Disbanded by AO 61/20.

115. Shepton Mallet Grammar School Cadet Corps: Rec. 7.10.17 (Somerset) (AO 360/17) and aff. to 3rd Bn. Somerset Volunteer Regt. Transferred to 4th Bn. Somerset Light Infantry by AO 116/20. Disbanded by AO 483/22.

116. Sherborne Cadet Company, 2nd, The Boys Brigade: Rec. 21.1.18 (Dorset) (AO 149/18).

117. Shifnal Cadet Company, Church Lads Brigade: Rec. 17.2.19 (Shropshire) (AO 137/19).

118. Shoreham Grammar School Cadet Corps: Rec. 10.10.21 (Sussex) (AO 527/21) and aff. to 4th Bn. Royal Sussex Regt.

119. Shropshire Light Infantry, King's, 1st Cadet Battalion: No 2 Company rec. 1.7.15 (AO 261/15). **No 3** Company rec. 1.7.15 (AO 261/15). **No 4** Company rec. 1.7.15 (AO 261/15). **No 5** Company rec. 1.7.15 (AO 302/15), disbanded by AO 265/22. **No 6** Company rec. 1.7.15 (AO 302/15), disbanded by AO 265/22. **No 7** Company rec. 31.7.15 (AO 430/15). **No 8** Company rec. 22.7.15 (AO 343/15), disbanded by AO 265/22. **No 9** Company rec. 5.7.15 (AO 302/15). **No 10** Company rec. 27.8.15 (AO 381/15), disbanded by AO 265/22. **No 11** Company rec. 27.8.15 (AO 381/15), disbanded by AO 265/22. **No 12** Company rec. 25.8.15 (AO 430/15). **No 13** Company rec. 21.12.17 (AO 111/18), became **No 1 Company, 2nd Cadet Bn. KSLI** by AO 209/18. Battalion aff. to 4th KSLI and admin. by Shropshire TFA.

120. Shropshire Light Infantry, King's, 2nd Cadet Battalion: No 1 Company rec. 21.12.17 (AO 111/18) as **No 13 Company, 1st Cadet Bn. KSLI.** Redes. by AO 209/18. **No 2 Company** rec. 1.5.18 (AO 209/18). **No 3 Company** rec. 15.5.19 (AO 251/19), disbanded by AO 265/22. Battalion aff. to 4th Bn. KSLI and admin. by Shropshire TFA.

121. Sidmouth Cadet Company, Church Lads Brigade: Rec. 11.12.12 (Devon) (AO 13/13).

122. Simon Langton School (Canterbury) Cadet Corps: Rec. 8.10.15 (Kent) (AO 23/16) and aff. to 4th Bn. East Kent Regt. Absorbed into Kent Public Secondary Schools Cadet Bn. by AO 137/19.

123. Sir Anthony Browne's School (Brentwood Cadets): Rec. 26.1.18 (Essex) (AO 149/18) and aff. to 4th Bn. Essex Regt. Inc. to four companies and redes. **12th Cadet Bn. (Sir Anthony Brown's School), Essex Regt.** by AO 265/22.

124. Sir Walter St. John's School Cadet Corps: Rec. 2.2.11 (County of London) (AO 161/11). Inc. to three companies by AO 340/19. Reduced to two companies by AO 310/22.

125. Sleaford Grammar School Cadet Corps: Rec. 5.4.19 (Lincoln) (AO 219/19). Aff. to 4th Bn. Lincolnshire Regt. by AO 25/21.

126. Slough Secondary School Cadets: Rec. 1.2.15 (Bucks) (AO 109/15) and aff. to the Buckinghamshire Bn. Ox and Bucks Light Infantry.

127. Somerset Light Infantry, 1st Cadet Corps, 4th Battalion: Rec. 27.3.17 (Somerset) (AO 168/177). Inc. to three companies by AO 419/19.

128. Somerset Light Infantry, 2nd Cadet Corps, 4th Battalion: Rec. 11.7.17 (Somerset) (AO 275/17).

129. Somerset Light Infantry, 1st Cadet Corps, 5th Battalion: Rec. 18.2.16 (Somerset) (AO 96/16).

130. Somerset Light Infantry, 2nd Cadet Corps, 5th Battalion: See 1st Cadet Corps, 1st Volunteer Bn. Somerset L.I.

131. Somerset Light Infantry, 3rd Cadet Corps, 5th Battalion: See 2nd Cadet Corps, 1st Volunteer Bn. Somerset L.I.

132. Somerset Light Infantry, 1st Cadet Corps, 1st Volunteer Battalion: Rec. 10.6.18 (Somerset) (AO 240/18). Redes. **2nd Cadet Corps, 5th Bn. Somerset L.I.** by AO 116/20.

133. Somerset Light Infantry, 2nd Cadet Corps, 1st Volunteer Battalion: Rec. 14.8.18 (Somerset) (AO 307/18). Redes. **3rd Cadet Corps, 5th Bn. Somerset L.I.** by AO 116/20.

134. Somerset Naval Cadet Corps, 1st: Rec. 16.12.12 (Somerset) (AO 13/13). Rec. withdrawn by AO 381/15.

135. Southall County School Cadet Company: Rec. 1.3.15 (Middlesex) (AO 139/15) and aff. to 8th Bn. Middlesex Regt. Became part of 2nd Cadet Bn. Middlesex Regt. by AO 96/16.

136. Southampton, King Edward VI School Cadet Corps: See King Edward Vi School (Southampton).

137. South Bank (Cadet) Company, 1st, The Boys Brigade: Rec. 1.12.21 (North Yorks) (AO 265/22).

138. Southend High School Cadet Corps: See Southend Technical School.

139. Southend Technical School Cadet Corps: Rec. 15.6.10 (Essex) (AO 197/10) and aff. to 6th Bn. Essex Regt. Redes. **Southend High School** by AO 274/13. Redes. **7th Cadet Bn. Essex Regt.** and inc. to four companies by AO 275/17. Reduced to two companies by AO 150/22.

140. South Essex Company, 17th, The Boys Brigade (East Ham Cadets): Rec. 16.12.12 (Essex) (AO 86/13). Rec. withdrawn by AO 373/13.

141. Southlands Grammar School Cadet Corps: Rec. 25.9.16 (Kent) (AO 375/16) and aff. to 5th Bn. East Kent Regt.

142. South London Cadets: Rec. 30.4.13 (County of London) (AO 235/13) and aff. to 21st Bn. London Regt. Amal. with 1st Cadet Bn. 10th Bn. London Regt. to form, **1st Bn. Lambeth Cadet Corps** by AO 24/20.

143. Southport Cadet Corps: Rec. 24.4.12 (West Lancs) (AO 207/12) and aff. to 7th Bn. King's Liverpool Regt.

144. Southsea Cadet Company, 1st, The Boys Brigade: Rec. 7.9.18 (Southampton) (AO 31/19). Rec. withdrawn by AO 60/20.

145. South Shields (Cadet) Company, 3rd, The Boys Brigade: Rec. 14.5.21 (Durham) (AO 271/21).

146. South Shields (Cadet) Company, 7th, The Boys Brigade: Rec. 14.4.22 (Durham) (AO 310/22).

147. South Shields (Cadet) Company, 8th, The Boys Brigade: Rec. 14.5.21 (Durham) (AO 271/21).

148. South Shields High School Cadet Corps: Rec. 8.5.18 (Durham) (AO 342/18) and aff. to 4th Northumbrian (Howitzer) Brigade RFA. Disbanded by AO 317/20.

149. South Staffordshire Regt.,1st Cadet Battalion, 2nd Volunteer Battalion: Rec. 13.4.18 (Stafford) (AO 173/18). Disbanded by AO 116/20.

150. Southwark Cadet Battalion, 1st, Church Lads Brigade: Rec. 19.1.12 (County of London) (AO 143/12). Reduced to six companies by AO 198/22.

151. Southwark Cadet Battalion, 2nd, Church Lads Brigade: Rec. 19.1.12 (County of London) (AO 143/12). Reduced to four companies by AO 198/22.

152. Southwark Cadet Battalion, 4th, Church Lads Brigade: Rec. 8.7.12 (Surrey) (AO 233/12).

153. Southwark Cadet Battalion, 5th, Church Lads Brigade: Rec. 17.10.11 (County of London) (AO 347/11). Reduced to two companies by AO 198/22.

154. Southwark Cadet Battalion, 7th, Church Lads Brigade: Rec. 12.1.14 (Surrey) (AO 38/14). Absorbed Redhill and Nutfield Company, CLB upon formation. Reduced to three companies by AO 150/22.

155. Southwark Cadet Battalion, 8th, Church Lads Brigade: Rec. 11.9.11 (Surrey) (AO 347/11). Reduced to four companies by AO 150/22.

156. Southwark Cadet Battalion, 9th, Church Lads Brigade: Rec. 19.6.12 (County of London) (AO 260/12). Reduced to two companies by AO 198/22. Reduced to one company by AO 310/22.

157. Southwark Cadet Battalion, 10th, Church Lads Brigade: Rec. 12.2.12 (Surrey) (AO 75/12). Reduced to one company by AO 150/22.

158. Southwell Cadet Battalion, 1st, Church Lads Brigade: Rec. 9.10.14 (Nottingham) (AO 451/14).

159. Southwell Cadet Battalion, 4th, Church Lads Brigade: Rec. 6.7.14 (Derby) (AO 416/14).

160. Southwell Cadet Battalion, 5th, Church Lads Brigade: Rec. 2.12.18 (Derby) (AO 31/19). Absorbed St. Barabas, Anne and John's Derby Cadet Company CLB and St. Paul's Derby Cadet Company CLB upon formation.

161. South West London Cadet Battalion: See St. Thomas's (Wandsworth).

162. S.S. Martin and Edmund Cadet Company, Salisbury Regiment Church Lads Brigade: Rec. 27.1.13 (Wilts) (AO 86/13). Redes. **Salisbury Company, Salisbury Regiment CLB** by AO 121/13. Amal. with 3rd Salisbury Cadet Corps CLB to form **1st Salisbury (Wiltshire) Cadet Battalion CLB** by AO 340/19.

163. Stafford Cadet Corps: Rec. 2.6.15 (Stafford) (AO 261/15) and aff. to 6th Bn. North Staffordshirte Regt. Absorbed into 1st Cadet Bn. North Staffordshire Regt. by AO 360/17.

164. Stafford Grammar School Cadet Corps: Rec. 4.2.15 (Stafford) (AO 109/15) and aff. to 6th Bn. North Staffordshire Regt. Absorbed into 1st Cadet Bn. Secondary Schools (Staffordshire Regt.) by AO 373/18.

165. Staffordshire Cadet Battalion, 2nd, The Boys Brigade: Rec. 25.4.19 (Stafford) (AO 251/19).

166. Staffordshire Regt. See 1st Cadet Bn. Secondary Schools.

167. Stamford School Company: See 3rd Lincoln Cadet Bn.

168. Stanhope Institute Cadet Corps: Rec. 18.3.16 (County of London) (AO 160/16). Transfered to the City of London TFA by AO 149/18. Became part of 1st Cadet Bn. 4th Bn. London Regt. by AO 156/20.

169. Stanley House (Bridge of Allan) Cadet Corps: Rec. 11.1.16 (Stirling) (AO 62/16) and aff. to 7th Bn. Argyll and Sutherland Highlanders. Disbanded by AO 111/18.

170. Stationers' Company's School (Hornsey) Cadet Company: Rec. 31.5.15 (Middlesex) (AO 261/15) and aff. to 7th Bn. Middlesex Regt. Became part of 1st Cadet Bn. Middlesex Regt. by AO 96/16.

171. Stevenston Cadet Company, 1st, The Boys Brigade: Rec. 18.2.19 (Ayr) (AO 137/19).

172. Steyne School Cadet Corps: Rec. 14.4.13 (Sussex) (AO 187/13) and aff. to 1st Home Counties Brigade RFA.

173. Stirling Boys Brigade Cadet Company, 1st: Rec. 2.5.22 (Stirling) (AO 310/22).

174. Stirling Company, 4th, Boys Brigade Cadets: Rec. 2.5.22 (Stirling) (AO 265/22).

175. Stirling Cadet Companies, 1st, 2nd and 3rd: Rec. 4.9.17 (Stirling) (AO 360/17) and aff. to 1st Bn. Stirlingshire Volunteer Regt. Became part of 1st Stirlingshire Cadet Bn. by AO 31/19.

176. Stirlingshire Cadet Battalion, 1st: Formed by AO 31/19 and the amal. of 1st, 2nd, 3rd Stirling Cadet Companies and the Campsie Cadet Company. Admin. by Stirling TFA and aff. to 1st Stirlingshire Volunteer Regt. Transfered to 7th Bn. Argyll and Sutherland Highlanders by AO 116/20.

177. Stockport Cadet Company, 3rd, The Boys Brigade: Rec. 25.7.22 (Chester) (AO 310/22).

178. Stockton-on-Tees Cadet Company, 1st, The Boys Brigade: Rec. 18.11.20 (Durham) (AO 25/21).

179. Stoke Farm School Cadet Corps: Rec. 9.8.20 (Worcs) (AO 406/20) and aff. to 8th Bn. Worcestershire Regt.

180. Stortford College Company: See 5thHertfordshire Cadets.

181. Stortford School Company: See 3rd Hertfordshire Cadets.

182. Stourport Cadet Company: Rec. 20.10.17 (Worcs) (AO 51/18) and aff. to 1st Bn. Worcestershire Volunteer Regt. Transfered to 7th Bn. Worcestershire Regt. by AO 116/20. Disbanded by AO 459/20.

183. Stowmarket Cadet Company, 1st, The Boys Brigade: Rec. 7.11.18 (Suffolk) (AO 31/19). Redes. **Mid-Suffolk Cadet Battalion, The Boys Brigade:** and inc. to ten companies by AO 118/21.

184. Strand School (Brixton) Cadet Corps: Rec. 13.5.15 (County of London) (AO 261/15) and aff. to 15th Bn. London Regt. Inc. to five companies by AO 310/22.

185. Stroud Cadet Corps: Rec. 17.6.18 (Gloucester) (AO 240/18) and aff. to 4th Bn. Gloucestershire Volunteer Regt. Disbanded by AO 24/20.

186. Styal Schools Cadet Company, Church Lads Brigade: Rec. 22.2.21 (East Lancs) (AO 271/21). Inc. to two companies and redes. **"Corps"** by AO 323/21.

187. Sudbury Grammar School Cadet Corps: Rec. 2.6.19 (Suffolk) (AO 251/19) and aff. to 5th Bn. Suffolk Regt.

188. Suffolk Regt.,1st Cadet Battalion: Rec. 1.6.16 (Suffolk) (AO 229/16) and aff. to 6th Bn. Disbanded by AO 72/21.

189. Suffolk Regt.,2nd Cadet Battalion: Rec. 18.10.17 (Suffolk) (AO 51/18) and aff. to 5th Bn. Disbanded by AO 493/21.

190. Suffolk Regt.,3rd Cadet Battalion: Rec. 10.6.18 (Suffolk) (AO 240/18) and aff. to 4th Bn. Disbanded by AO 452/12.

191. Sunbury House School Cadet Company: Rec. 10.7.12 (Middlesex) (AO 260/12) and aff. to 9th Bn. Middlesex Regt. Became part of 3rd Cadet Bn. Middlesex Regt. by AO 96/16.

192. Surrey Cadet Battalion, 1st, The Boys Brigade: See 1st Reigate Cadets

193. Surrey Volunteer Regt.,1st Cadet Company, 2nd Battalion: Rec. 12.11.17 (Surrey) (AO 51/18). Became part of 4th Cadet Bn. Royal West Surrey Regt. by AO 103/19.

194. Surrey Yeomanry, "E" Cadet Squadron: Rec. 9.12.12 (Surrey) (AO 49/13). Disbanded 28.1.16 (AO 96/16).

195. Sussex Regt.,Royal, 5th Battalion, 2nd Cadet Battalion: Rec. 16.4.17 (Sussex) (AO 111/18). Transfered to 44th Home Counties Divisional Royal Engineers by AO 323/21. Disbanded by AO 527/21.

196. Sussex Volunteer Regt.,No 1 Company, 3rd Battalion: Rec. 31.12.17 (Sussex) (AO 111/18). Absorbed into 2nd Chichester Cadet Bn. CLB 21.4.19 (AO 251/19).

197. Sussex Volunteer Regt.,No 2 Company, 3rd Battalion: Rec. 4.1.18 (Sussex) (AO 173/18). Disbanded by AO 24/20.

198. Sussex Volunteer Regt.,4th Battalion Cadet Company: Rec. 4.2.18 (Sussex) (AO 173/18). Disbanded by AO 24/20.

199. Sussex Volunteer Regt.,No 1 Company, 6th Battalion: Rec. 5.4.18 (Sussex) (AO 173/18). Disbanded by AO 219/19.

200. Sussex Volunteer Regt.,No 1 Company, 9th Battalion: Rec. 3.4.18 (Sussex) (AO 173/18).

201. Sussex Yeomanry Cadets: See Brighton Brigade, Sussex Cadets.

202. Sutton County School Cadet Corps: Rec. 14.6.15 (Surrey) (AO 343/15) and aff. to 5th Bn. East Surrey Regt. Became part of 3rd Cadet Bn. Royal West Surrey Regt. by AO 103/19.

203. Sutton High School Cadet Corps: Rec. 13.9.15 (Surrey) (AO 403/15). Aff. to 5th Bn. East Surrey Regt. by AO 23/16. Became part of 3rd Cadet Bn. Royal West Surrey Regt. by AO 103/19.

204. Swansea Grammar School Cadet Corps: Rec. 22.3.17 (Glamorgan) (AO 168/17) and aff. to 6th Bn. Welsh Regt. Disbanded by AO 156/20.

205. Swinton Schools Cadet Company: Rec. 4.11.21 (East Lancs) (AO 265/22) and aff. to 8th Bn. Manchester Regt.

T

1. Tamworth Cadet Company, Church Lads Brigade: Rec. 27.3.17 (Stafford) (AO 168/17). Disbanded by AO 116/20.

2. Tamworth Grammar School Cadet Corps: Rec. 17.7.15 (Stafford) (AO 302/15) and aff. to 6th Bn. North Staffordshire Regt. Transfered to the 2nd Bn. Staffordshire Volunteer Regt. by AO 51/18. Absorbed into 1st Cadet Bn. Secondary Schools (Staffordshire Regt.) by AO 373/18.

3. Tamworth Volunteer Cadet Corps: Rec. 15.11.17 (Stafford) (AO 51/18) and aff. to 2nd Bn. Staffordshire Volunteer Regt. Disbanded by AO 493/21.

4. Taunton's School (Southampton) Cadet Company: Rec. 31.1.16 (Southampton) (AO 96/16) and aff. to 5th Bn. Hampshire Regt. Redes. "Corps" by AO 406/16. Amal. with Southampton, King Edward VI School to form **5th Hampshire Regt. Cadet Bn.** by AO 307/18.

5. Tavistock Grammar School Cadet Corps: Rec. 12.12.17 (Devon) (AO 111/18) and aff. to 5th Bn. Devonshire Regt.

6. Temple Grove (Eastbourne) Cadet Corps: Rec. 5.3.15 (Sussex) (AO 225/15) and aff. to 4th Bn. Royal Sussex Regt.

7. Tenison Grammar School Cadet Corps: Rec. 14.10.15 (County of London) (AO 457/15) and aff. to 16th Bn. London Regt.

8. Thames Valley (Kingston) Company, 9th Boys Brigade Cadets: Rec. 13.1.19 (Surrey) (AO 103/19). Became part of 1st Surrey Cadet Bn. The Boys Brigade by AO 61/20.

9. Tideswell Cadet Company, Church Lads Brigade: Rec. 8.1.17 (Derby) (AO 65/17). Disbanded by AO 95/22.

10. Tideswell Grammar School Cadet Corps: Rec. 5.11.18 (Derby) (AO 31/19) and aff. to 5th Volunteer Bn. Notts and Derby Regt. Absorbed into the Derbyshire Schools Cadet Bn. by AO 219/19.

11. Tiffin School (Kingston-on-Thames) Cadet Corps: Rec. 11.10.15 (Surrey) (AO 430/15) and aff. to 6th Bn. East Surrey Regt. Became part of 1st Cadet Bn. East Surrey Regt. by AO 103/19.

12. Tiverton Cadet Company, Church Lads Brigade: Rec. 2.1.12 (Devon) (AO 41/12). Disbanded by AO 29/23.

13. Todmorden Cadet Company, Church Lads Brigade: Rec. 21.2.22 (East Lancs) (AO 265/22).

14. Tollington School Cadet Company: Rec. 18.9.11 (Middlesex) (AO 316/11). Became part of 1st Cadet Bn. Middlesex Regt. by AO 96/16.

15. Torquay Cadet Company: Rec. 1.8.16 (Devon) (AO 302/16) and aff. to Devon (Fortress) Engineers.

16. Totnes Cadet Company: Rec. 21.5.15 (Devon) (AO 225/15) and aff. to 5th Bn. Devonshire Regt. Disbanded by AO 493/21.

17. Tower Hamlets Cadets: See Rutland Street School.

18. Tranet Industrial School Cadet Corps: Rec. 20.11.12 (Haddington) (AO 13/13) and aff. to 8th Bn. Royal Scots. Transfered to 57th (Lowland) Medium Brigade RGA by AO 72/21.

19. Trinity Mission Boys' Club Cadets: Rec. 3.11.14 (County of London) (AO 79/15). Disbanded 31.12.15 (AO 406/16).

20. Tynemouth Cadet Company, 1st, The Boys Brigade: Rec. 29.5.19 (Northumberland) (AO 419/19). Disbanded by AO 226/21.

21. Tynemouth Cadet Company, 3rd, The Boys Brigade: Rec. 3.2.20 (Northumberland) (AO 406/20).

22. Tynemouth Cadet Company, 4th, The Boys Brigade: Rec. 28.4.21 (Northumberland) (AO 365/21).

23. Tynemouth Cadet Company, 5th, The Boys Brigade: Rec. 27.4.22 (Northumberland) (AO 256/22).

U

1. Uddington Cadet Company: Rec. by AO 168/17 (Lanark) and added to the 1st Lanarkshire Cadet Bn.

2. University School, Hastings Cadet Company: Rec. 10.10.10 (Sussex) (AO 281/10) and aff. to 2nd Home Counties Field Company, Royal Engineers.

3. Upper Tooting School Cadet Corps: Rec. 26.1.14 (City of London) (AO 63/14). Redes. **Balham and Upper Tooting Cadet Company** by AO 275/17.

4. Ushaw Cadet Corps: Rec. 6.5.18 (Durham) (AO 209/18). Disbanded by AO 116/20.

5. Usk Territorial Cadet Corps: Rec. 1.7.10 (Monmouth) (AO 197/10) and aff. to 2nd Bn. Monmouthshire Regt. Became part of 1st Cadet Bn. Monmouthshire Regt. by AO 233/12.

V

1. Ventnor Cadet Company: Rec. 28.4.11 (Southampton) (AO 161/11) and aff. to 8th Bn. Hampshire Regt. Absorbed into 3rd Cadet (Isle of Wight) Bn. Hampshire Regt. by AO 457/15.

W

1. Wagon Works Cadet Corps: Rec. 17.6.18 (Gloucester) (AO 240/18) and aff. to 3rd Bn. Gloucestershire Volunteer Regt. Disbanded by AO 25/21.

2. Wakefield Cadet Battalion, Church Lads Brigade: Rec. 19.6.12 (West Yorks) (AO 207/12).

3. Wakefield Grammar School Cadet Corps: Rec. 13.4.17 (West Yorks) (AO 275/17) and aff. to 4th Bn. Yorkshire Light Infantry.

4. Walkeringham Cadet Company: Rec. 9.11.16 (Nottingham) (AO 406/16). Disbanded by AO 209/18.

5. Wallace Hall Academy (Closeburn) Cadet Corps: Rec. 3.12.16 (Dumfries) (AO 65/17) and aff. to 5th Bn. King's Own Scottish Borderers. Disbanded by AO 156/20.

6. Wallaset Cadet Corps: See 3rd New Brighton Cadet Corps.

7. Walsall Catholic Cadets: Rec. 19.4.20 (Stafford) (AO 555/20) and aff. to 5th Bn. South Staffordshire Regt.

8. Waltham Abbey Cadet Corps: Rec. 13.11.18 (Essex) (AO 69/19) and aff. to 2nd Volunteer Bn. Essex Regt. Transfered to 4th Bn. by AO 116/20. Transfered to 1st Bn. Hertfordshire Regt. and the admin. of the Herts TFA by AO 229/22.

9. Walthamstow and Leyton Cadets: See Walthamstow Cadets.

10. Walthamstow Cadets: Rec. 23.12.14 (Essex) (AO 79/15) and aff. to 7th Bn. Essex Regt. Redes. **Walthamstow and Leyton Cadets** by AO 343/15. Disbanded by AO 219/19.

11. Walton House School Cadet Corps: Rec. 23.11.22 (Wilts) (AO 483/22) and aff. to 4th Bn. Wiltshire Regt.

12. Wandsworth Boys Naval Brigade: Rec. 17.10.11 (County of London) (AO 11/12). Transfered to the admin. of the Admiralty by AO 116/20.

13. Wandsworth Cadet Company, (St. Thomas's): See St. Thomas's, Wandsworth.

14. Wandsworth Scottish Scouts: Rec. 11.7.16 (County of London) (AO 262/16) and aff. to 14th Bn. London Regt. Redes. **Wandsworth Scottish Cadet Corps** by AO 137/19. Inc. to three companies by AO 340/19. Reduced to two companies by AO 198/22. Rec. withdrawn by AO 435/22.

15. Wandsworth Technical Institute Cadet Corps: Rec . 14.7.15 (County of London) (AO 343/15). Inc. to two companies by AO 310/22.

16. Waring Cadet Corps: Rec. 24.12.10 (County of London) (AO 130/11). Disbanded by AO 116/20.

17. Warley Company, 1st, The Boys Brigade Cadets: Rec. 6.6.19 (Essex) (AO 276/19).

18. Warley Garrison Cadets: Rec. 6.10.11 (Essex) (AO 316/11). Disbanded 4.10.15 (AO 430/15).

19. Warminster Cadet Company: Rec. 29.8.14 (Wilts) (AO 416/14) and aff. to 4th Bn. Wiltshire Regt. Disbanded by AO 483/22.

20. Warren Farm School Cadet Corps: Rec. 10.10.21 (Sussex) (AO 527/21) and aff. to 4th Bn. Royal Sussex Regt.

21. Warrington Grammar School Cadet Corps: Rec. 11.2.15 (West Lancs) (AO 225/15) and aff. to 4th Bn. South Lancashire Regt.

22. Warrington League of the Cross Boys Brigade: Rec. 1.6.13 (West Lancs) (AO 337/13). Disbanded by AO 95/17.

23. Warwickshire Cadet Army Service Corps: Rec. 23.4.18 (Warwick) (AO 173/18) and aff. to South Midland Divisional HQ Company ASC. Redes. **Warwickshire Royal Field Artillery Cadets** and transferred to 68th Brigade RFA by AO 72/21.

24. Warwickshire Cadet Machine Gun Company: Rec. 30.1.17 (Warwick) (AO 95/17). Amal. with Warwickshire Old Boys Cadet Corps by AO 340/19.

25. Warwickshire Cadet Signal Company: Rec. 19.2.17 (Warwick) (AO 128/17) and aff. to Southern Signal Company RE. Disbanded by AO 72/21.

26. Warwickshire Old Boys Cadet Corps: Rec. 14.5.18 (Warwick) (AO 209/18) and aff. to 5th Bn. Royal Warwickshire Regt. Amal. with Warwickshire Cadet Machine Gun Company by AO 340/19. Disbanded by AO 527/21.

27. Warwickshire Regt.,Royal, 1st Cadet Battalion: Rec. 15.6.10 (Warwick) (AO 258/10) and aff. to 8th Bn. **Sutton Coldfield Company** transfered to 3rd Cadet Bn. Royal Warwickshire Regt. by AO 261/51.

28. Warwickshire Regt.,Royal, 2nd Cadet Battalion: Rec. 21.6.10 (Warwick) (AO 258/10) and aff. to 7th Bn. Reduced to four companies by AO 61/20.

29. Warwickshire Regt.,Royal, 3rd Cadet Battalion: Rec. 4.3.14 (Warwick) (AO 261/15) and formed by the amal. of Bablake School, King Edward's Camp Hill, King Edward's (Aston), St. Philip's Grammar School, Leamington Municipal School, Yardley Secondary School, Waverley Road School and the Sutton Coldfield Company of the 1st Cadet Bn. Royal Warwickshire Regt. Absorbed King Edward VI School (Nuneaton) and King Edward VI School (Stratford-on-Avon) cadet units and redes. **3rd (Schools) Cadet Bn.** by AO 160/16. Reduced to six companies by AO 493/21. Reduced to four companies by AO 527/21. "C" and "D" (King Edward's Grammar School, Aston) Companies disbanded by AO 265/22. "A" and "B" (King Edward's School, Camp Hill) Companies disbanded by AO 310/22. Waverley Road School Company disbanded by AO 29/23.

30. Warwickshire Regt.,Royal, 4th (Schools) Cadet Battalion: Rec. 4.3.14 (Warwick) (AO 160/16) and aff. to 6th Bn. Absorbed King Edward's Grammar School (Five Ways) Cadet Corps upon formation. Reduced to seven companies by AO 452/21.

31. Warwickshire Royal Field Artillery Cadets: See Warwickshire ASC Cadets.

32. Warwickshire Yeomanry, 1st Cadet Battalion: Rec. 7.11.10 (Warwick) (AO 11/11). Rec. withdrawn 31.12.13 (AO 10/14).

33. Watford Grammar School Company: See 6th Hertfordshire Cadets.

34. Watford Scouts: See 2nd Hertfordshire Cadets.

35. Waverley Road Secondary School (Birmingham) Cadet Corps: Rec. 29.4.15 (Warwick) (AO 225/15). Absorbed into 3rd Cadet Bn. Royal Warwickshire Regt. by AO 261/15. Disbanded by AO 29/23.

36. Wedmore Cadet Corps: Rec. 31.7.15 (Somerset) (AO 343/15) and aff. to 4th Bn. Somerset Light Infantry. Redes. **"Sexeys" School (Blackford) Cadet Corps** by AO 24/20.

37. Welbeck Cadet Battalion: Rec. 19.8.14 (Nottingham) (AO 416/14) and aff. to 8th Bn. Notts and Derby Regt.

38. Wells Boys Blue School Cadet Company: Rec. 1.6.18 (Somerset) (AO 240/18) and aff. to 3rd Bn. Somerset Volunteer Regt. Transfered to 4th Bn. Somerset Light Infantry by AO 116/20.

39. Welsh Fusiliers, Royal, 5th Battalion, 1st Cadet Battalion: Formed by AO 240/18 and the amal. of Mold, Hawarden and Rhyl County Schools, St. Asaph School and Epworth College cadet units. Admin. by Flint TFA.

40. Welsh Fusiliers, Royal, 1st Cadet (Dolgelly County School) Company, 7th Battalion: Rec. 13.1.15 (Merioneth) (AO 139/15). Redes. **1st Cadet (Newtown County School) Company** by AO 219/19.

41. Wessex Cadet Battalion, 1st, The Boys Brigade: Rec. 7.11.17 (Somerset) (AO 51/18).

42. West Bromwich Municipal Secondary School Cadet Corps: Rec. 1.6.15 (Stafford) (AO 261/15) and aff. to 5th (Staffordshire) Battery, RFA. Absorbed into 1st Cadet Bn., Secondary Schools (Staffordshire Regt.) by AO 373/18.

43. Westcliff High School Cadet Corps: Rec. 1.1.22 (Essex) (AO 355/22) and aff. to 6th Bn. Essex Regt.

44. West Croydon Cadets: Rec. 19.5.13 (Surrey) (AO 187/13) and aff. to 4th Bn. Royal West Surrey Regt.

45. West End (Ravenscourt Park) Cadet Corps: Rec. 23.1.17 (County of London) (AO 95/17) and aff. to 13th Bn. London Regt. Disbanded by AO 116/20.

46. Westerham and Chipstead Cadet Corps: Rec. 4.11.10 (Kent) (AO 65/11) and aff. to 4th Bn. Royal West Kent Regt.

47. West Ham Cadet Corps: Rec. 9.5.18 (Essex) (AO 240/18) and aff. to 1st Bn. Essex Volunteer Regt. Transfered to 6th Bn. Essex Regt. by AO 116/20. Disbanded by AO 211/20.

48. West Ham Cadets ("A" Company, 1st Cadet Bn. Essex Regt.): Rec. 22.6.10 (Essex) (AO 197/20) and aff. to 6th Bn. Essex Regt. Became part of 1st Cadet Bn. by AO 65/11.

49. West Hoathly Cadet Company: Rec. 9.1.22 (Sussex) (AO 265/22) and aff. to 4th Bn. Royal Sussex Regt.

50. West Kent (Tunbridge Wells) Cadet Company, 12th, The Boys Brigade: Rec. 20.9.17 (Kent)) (AO 111/18). Disbanded by AO 219/19.

51. West Kent (Bexley Heath) Cadet Company, 14th, The Boys Brigade: Rec. 20.9.17 (Kent) (AO 111/18).

52. West Kent Regt.,Royal, 1st Cadet Battalion: Rec. 12.8.13 (Kent) (AO 337/13) and aff. to 5th Bn.

53. West Kent Regt.,Royal, 2nd Cadet Battalion: Rec. 10.8.18 (Kent) (AO 342/18) and aff. to 4th Bn. Inc. to five companies by AO 24/20.

54. West Lancashire (Liverpool) Cadet Battalion, Catholic Boys Brigade: Rec. 1.6.14 (West Lancs) (AO 218/14). Rec. withdrawn by AO 156/20.

55. West Lewisham Cadet Corps: See 1st Cadet Bn. 17th Bn. London Volunteer Regt.

56. Westminster Battalion, Catholic Boys Brigade: Rec. 19.10.14 (County of London) (AO 79/15). Redes. **The Catholic Cadets** by AO 251/19. Reduced to four companies by AO 310/22.

57. Westoe Secondary School Cadet Corps: Rec. 22.3.18 (Durham) (AO 209/18).

58. Weston Point Cadet Corps: Rec. 21.3.18 (Chester) (AO 173/18) and aff. to 5th Bn. Chershire Regt. Inc. to two companies by AO 373/18.

59. Weston Training School Cadet Corps: Rec. 14.4.16 (Warwick) (AO 188/16) and aff. to 7th Bn. Royal Warwickshire Regt.

60. West Riding Regt.,5th Battalion Cadet Battalion: Rec. 8.6.15 (West Yorks) (AO 343/15).

61. West Riding Regt.,6th Battalion Cadet Battalion: See Settle Cadet Bn.

62. West Surrey Cadets: Rec. 8.8.10 (Surrey) (AO 225/10) and aff. to 5th Bn. Royal West Surrey Regt. Rec. withdrawn by AO 233/12 for all except the Farnham portion of the unit which was redes. **The Farnham Company, West Surrey Cadets.** Redes. "G" and "H" (Surrey) Companies, 1st Cadet Bn. of Hampshire by AO 274/13. Redes. "F" and "G" (Surrey) Companies by AO 95/17. Redes. "E" (Surrey) Company, 1/4th Hampshire Regt. Cadet Bn. by AO 307/18. Redes. Farnham Cadet Corps (The Queen's) and aff. to 5th Bn. Royal West Surrey Regt. by AO 25/21.

63. West Surrey Regt.,Royal, 1st Cadet Battalion: Rec. 2.2.11 (County of London) (AO 102/11). Redes. 1st Cadet Bn. The London Regt. (The Queen's) by AO 161/11. Aff. to 24th Bn. London Regt. by AO 555/20.

64. West Surrey Regt.,Royal, 1st Cadet Battalion: Rec. 19.7.15 (Surrey) (AO 381/15) and aff. to 4th Bn. Absorbed Whitgift Middle School and Croydon High School cadet units by AO 103/19.

65. West Surrey Regt.,Royal, 2nd Cadet Battalion: Rec. 21.10.18 (Surrey) (AO 103/19) and formed by the amal. of St. George's College (Weybridge), Woking County School, Dorking High School and Farnham Grammar School cadet units. Aff. to 5th Bn. Absorbed Cordwalles Cadet Company by AO 24/20. Reduced to four companies by AO 198/22.

66. West Surrey Regt.,Royal, 3rd Cadet Battalion: Rec. 21.10.18 (Surrey) (AO 103/19) and formed by the amal. of Sutton County School, Sutton High School, Purley County School and Russell Hill cadet units. Aff. to 4th Bn.

67. West Surrey Regt.,Royal, 4th Cadet Battalion: Rec. 21.10.18 (Surrey) (AO 103/19) and formed by the amal. of 1st Cadet Corps, 2nd Bn. Surrey Volunteer Regt., Caterham Cadet Corps, Bletchingley and Godstone Cadet Corps and 3rd Volunteer Bn. Royal West Surrey Regt. Cadet Corps. Aff. to 5th Bn. Reduced to three companies by AO 24/20. Aff. transferred to 4th Bn. by AO 371/20. Rec. withdrawn by AO 323/21.

68. West Surrey Regt.,Royal,3rd Volunteer Battalion Cadet Corps: Rec. 4.3.18 (Surrey) (AO 149/18). Absorbed into 4th Cadet Bn. Royal West Surrey Regt. by AO 103/19.

69. West Yorkshire Regt., "C" Cadet Company, 7th Battalion: Rec. 1.1.16 (AO 125/16). Disbanded by AO 156/20.

70. Weybridge and District Scout Cadets: Rec. 23.1.11 (Surrey) (AO 40/11) and aff. to 6th Bn. East Surrey Regt. Rec. withdrawn by AO 260/12.

71. Weybridge Park College Cadet Corps: See Highfield School Cadet Corps.

72. Weybridge Secondary School Cadets: Rec. 20.3.14 (Dorset) (AO 144/14). Aff. to 4th Bn. Dorset Regt. by AO 173/18. Inc. to two companies by AO 116/20.

73. Wheelwright Grammar School Cadet Corps: Rec. 26.3.17 (West Yorks) (AO 168/17) and aff. to 4th Bn. Yorkshire Light Infantry.

74. Whitchurch (Salop) Cadet Company, Church Lads Brigade: Rec. 1.11.12 (Shropshire) (AO 343/12).

75. White Cross Cadet Corps: Rec. 5.9.10 (Derby) (AO 258/10) and aff. to 6th Bn. Notts and Derby Regt. Rec. withdrawn 4.9.11 (AO 316/11).

76. Whitgift Middle School Cadet Corps: Rec. 13.12.15 (Surrey) (AO 23/16) and aff. to 4th Bn. Royal West Surrey Regt. Absorbed into 1st Cadet Bn. Royal West Surrey Regt. by AO 103/19.

77. Whitwell and Worksop Priory Cadet Company, Church Lads Brigade: See Whitwell, Welbeck and Chukney.

78. Whitwell, Welbeck and Chukney Cadet Company, Church Lads Brigade: Rec. 19.11.14 (Nottingham) (AO 111/18). Redes. **Whitwell and Worksop Priory** by AO 209/18.

79. Wickford Cadets: Rec. 21.4.17 (Essex) (AO 275/17) and aff. to 4th Bn. Essex Regt. Became part of 8th Cadet Bn. Essex Regt. by AO 209/18.

80. Willaston School (Nantwich) Cadet Corps: Rec. 7.9.15 (Chester) (AO 430/15). Aff. to 4th Bn. Cheshire Volunteer Regt. by AO 51/18.

81. Willey's Cadet Company: Rec. 19.6.18 (Devon) (AO 307/18) and aff. to Devon (Fortress) Engineers.

82. Wiltshire Regt.,1st Volunteer Cadet Battalion: Rec. 10.4.18 (Wilts) (AO 173/18). Aff. to 4th Bn. Wiltshire Regt. by AO 116/20.

83. Wimbledon Boys Naval Brigade: Rec. 19.5.13 (Surrey) (AO 235/13). Amal. with Richmond Boys Naval Brigade to form **2nd Cadet Bn. East Surrey Regt.** by AO 103/19.

84. Wimbledon College Cadet Corps: Rec. 13.9.15 (Surrey) (AO 430/15) and aff. to 5th Bn. East Surrey Regt. Became part of 1st Cadet Bn. East Surrey Regt. by AO 103/19.

85. Wimbourne Grammar School Cadet Corps: Rec. 20.7.15 (Dorset) (AO 343/15) and aff. to 4th Bn. Dorset Regt.

86. Winchburgh (Cadet) Company, The Boys Brigade: Rec. 23.12.20 (Linlithgow) (AO 72/21). Transfered to the admin. of Midlothian TAA by AO 229/22.

87. Winchester Cadet Battalion, 1st, Church Lads Brigade: See Winchester Cadet Corps CLB.

88. Winchester Cadet Battalion, 2nd, Church Lads Brigade: Rec. 10.2.13 (Surrey) (AO 86/13). Inc. to five companies by AO 251/19. Redes. **Cranleigh Cadet Company CLB** by AO 514/20. New 2nd Battalion rec. 29.11.21 (AO 265/22). Inc. to four companies by AO 29/23.

89. Winchester Cadet Corps, Church Lads Brigade: Rec. 15.12.11 (Southampton) (AO 109/12). Redes. **1st Winchester Cadet Bn. CLB** by AO 233/12. Inc. to six companies by AO 276/19. Reduced to five companies by AO 435/22.

90. Windsor Cadet Company, 2nd, 4th Battalion Royal Berkshire Regt: Rec. 14.10.14 (Berks) (AO 511/14). Amal. with 3rd (Windsor) Cadet Company to form the **Windsor Cadet Companies** by AO 225/15.

91. Windsor Cadet Company, 3rd, 4th Battalion Royal Berkshire Regt: Rec. 17.4.15 (Berks) (AO 225/15). Amal. with 2nd (Windsor) Cadet Company to form the **Windsor Cadet Companies** by AO 225/15.

92. Windsor Cadet Companies, 4th Battalion Royal Berkshire Regt: Formed by the amal. of 2nd and 3rd (Windsor) Cadet Companies, 4th Bn. Royal Berkshire Regt. (AO 225/15) (Berks). Inc. to three companies by AO 323/21.

93. Wirksworth Grammar School Cadet Corps: Rec. 5.11.17 (Derby) (AO 51/18). Absorbed into Derbyshire Schools Cadet Bn. by AO 219/19.

94. Wisbech Grammar School Cadet Corps: Rec. 2.2.18 (Cambs and Ely) (AO 149/18) and aff. to 3rd Bn. Cambridgeshire Volunteer Regt. Transfered to 1st Bn. Cambridgeshire Regt. by AO 116/20.

95. Wishaw Cadet Corps: Rec. 20.7.17 (Lanark) (AO 51/18). Absorbed the Wishaw High School Cadet Corps by AO 219/19. Disbanded by AO 211/20.

96. Wishaw High School Cadet Corps: Rec. 18.8.16 (Lanark) (AO 95/17). Absorbed into Wishaw Cadet Corps by AO 219/19.

97. Witney Company, 1st, The Boys Brigade Cadet Corps: Rec. 14.10.20 (Oxford) (AO 514/20) and aff. to 4th Bn. Oxfordshire and Buckinghamshire Light Infantry. Redes. **1st Witney Cadet Corps, The Boys Brigade** and aff. to 4th Bn. Ox & Bucks cancelled by AO 25/21.

98. Woking County School Cadet Corps: Rec. 15.11.15 (Surrey) (AO 457/15) and aff. to 5th Bn. Royal West Surrey Regt. Became part of 2nd Cadet Bn. Royal West Surrey Regt. by AO 103/19.

99. Wokingham Cadet Company: Rec. 11.10.18 (Berks) (AO 373/18) and aff. to 4th Bn. Royal Berkshire Regt. Disbanded by AO 493/21.

100. Wolverley School Cadet Company: Rec. 12.2.15 (Worcs) (AO 139/15) and aff. to 7th Bn. Worcestershire Regt. Became part of Worcestershire Cadet Bn. by AO 188/16.

101. Woodhouse Grove School (Apperley Bridge) Cadet Corps: Rec. 4.3.15 (West Yorks) (AO 225/15). Aff. to 6th Bn. West Yorkshire Regt. by AO 261/15. Rec. withdrawn by AO 401/22.

102. Woodford Cadet Company: Rec. 12.5.15 (Essex) (AO 225/15) and aff. to 4th Bn. Essex Regt. Became part of 5th (Schools) Cadet Bn. Essex Regt. by AO 335/16.

103. Woodlands (Deganwy) School Cadet Corps: Rec. 1.12.15 (Carnarvon) (AO 23/16).

104. Woodstock Cadet Corps: Rec. 29.7.16 (Oxford) (AO 302/16) and aff. to 4th Bn. Oxfordshire and Buckinghamshire Light Infantry.

105. Woolwich Cadet Corps, 1st: Rec. 12.3.12 (County of London) (AO 143/12) and aff. to 2nd London Brigade RFA. Redes. **1st County of London Royal Engineer Cadets (Woolwich)** by AO 111/18. Disbanded by AO 452/21.

106. Woolwich Scout Cadet Corps, 2nd: Rec. 12.10.12 (County of London) (AO 187/13). Inc. to three companies by AO 340/19. Disbanded by AO 211/20.

107. Worcester Cadet Battalion: "A" Company rec. 13.4.18 (AO 173/18). "B" Company rec. 24.5.18 (AO 209/18). Both companies admin. by Worcs. TFA, aff. to 2nd Volunteer Bn. Worcestershire Regt. and disbanded by AO 219/19.

108. Worcester Cadet Battalion, 1st, Church Lads Brigade: Rec. 28.6.12 (Worcs) (AO 233/12).

109. Worcester Cadet Battalion, 2nd (Coventry), Church Lads Brigade: Rec. 7.11.11 (Warwick) (AO 144/14). Absorbed Alcester Cadet Company CLB by AO 381/15. Redes. 1st Coventry Cadet Bn. CLB by AO 276/19.

110. Worcestershire Cadet Battalion: Rec. 14.4.16 (Worcs) (AO 188/16) and formed by the amal. of Dudley Grammar School, Kidderminster Grammar School, King Edward School Stourbridge, Wolverley School, Bromsgrove School, Oldbury School and Halesowen Grammar School cadet units. Aff. to 7th Bn. Worcestershire Regt. Redes. 1st Cadet Bn. Worcestershire Regt. by AO 406/16. Absorbed Hartlebury Grammar School and Evesham Grammar School cadet units by AO 156/20. Reduced to eight companies by AO 255/20.

111. Worcestershire Cadet Signal Company: Rec. 1.10.20 (Worcs) (AO 184/21) and aff. to 48th (South Midland) Divisional Signal Company.

112. Worcestershire Regt.,1st Cadet Battalion: See Worcestershire Cadet Bn.

113. Worcestershire Regt.,2nd Cadet Battalion (Dudley Grammar School): Rec. 11.12.14 (Worcs) (AO 79/15) and aff. to 7th Bn. Worcestershire Regt. Redes. Dudley Grammar School Cadet Company by AO 139/15. Became part of Worcestershire Cadet Bn. by AO 188/16.

114. Worcestershire Regt.,3rd Cadet Battalion (Kidderminster Grammar School): Rec. 11.12.14 (Worcs) (AO 79/15) and aff. to 7th Bn. Worcestershire Regt. Redes. Kidderminster Grammar School Cadet Company by AO 139/15. Became part of Worcestershire Cadet Bn. by AO 188/16.

115. Wrington Cadet Company: Rec. 21.6.19 (Somerset) (AO 276/19) and aff. to 4th Bn. Somerset Light Infantry. Disbanded by AO 483/22.

116. Writtle Cadets: Rec. 13.9.16 (Essex) (AO 335/16) and aff. to 5th Bn. Essex Regt. Became part of 8th Cadet Bn. Essex Regt. by AO 51/18.

117. Wycliffe College (Stonehouse) Cadet Corps: Rec. 22.3.15 (Gloucester) (AO 225/15) and aff. to 5th Bn. Gloucestershire Regt. Disbanded by AO 493/21.

118. Wymondham Cadet Corps: Rec. 22.12.17 (Norfolk) (AO 111/18) and aff. to 4th Bn. Norfolk Regt.

Y

1. Yardley Secondary School Cadet Corps: Rec. 4.3.15 (Warwick) (AO 139/15). Absorbed into 3rd Cadet Bn. Royal Warwickshire Regt. by AO 261/15.

2. Yealmpton Cadet Corps: Rec. 15.3.11 (Devon) (AO 130/11) and aff. to Devon (Fortress) Engineers. Redes. No 1 (Yealmpton) Cadet Company, Devon (Fortress) Royal Engineers by AO 290/12. Rec. withdrawn by AO 323/21.

3. YMCA Junior Department Cadet Corps: Rec. 10.5.18 (East Lancs) (AO 240/18). Inc. to two companies by AO 61/20.

4. York Cadet Battalion, 1st, Church Lads Brigade: Rec. 19.8.14 (West Yorks) (AO 416/14). Transfered to the admin. of North Riding TAA by AO 355/22.

5. York Cadet Battalion, 2nd, Church Lads Brigade: Rec. 15.5.12 (East Yorks) (AO 233/12).

6. York Cadet Corps, 3rd, Church Lads Brigade: Rec. 15.1.15 (West Yorks) (AO 79/15). Redes. **"Battalion"** by AO 23/16.

7. York Cadet Battalion, 4th, Church Lads Brigade: Rec. 5.9.12 (West Yorks) (AO 290/12). Redes. **1st Sheffield Cadet Bn. CLB** by AO 457/15.

8. York Cadet Battalion, 5th, Church Lads Brigade: Rec. 1.1.12 (West Yorks) (AO 41/12). Redes. **2nd Sheffield Cadet Bn. CLB** by AO 457/15.

9. Yorkshire Regt.,4th Cadet Battalion: Formed by AO 116/20 and the amal. of Guisborough Grammar School, Scorton Grammar School and the 2/3rd North Riding Volunteer Regt. cadet units. Admin. by North Yorks TFA.

10. Yorkshire Regt.,5th Cadet Battalion: Formed by AO 116/20 and the amal. of Scarborough Municipal School, Elmfield College (York) and the 2nd Bn. North Riding Volunteer Regt. cadet units. Scarborough School portion disbanded by AO 401/22. Admin. by North Yorks TFA

11. Yorkshire Squadron, Imperial Yeomanry Cadets: Rec. 1.7.12 (West Yorks) (AO 260/12) and aff. to Yorkshire Hussars Yeomanry. Disbanded by AO 401/22.

Royal Artillery:

A 33. B 37, 67. C 2, 37, 54, 75. E 4, 10. F 23. G 19. H 2, 35, 60. I 7, 8, 16.
K 26. L 7, 21, 59. M 32. N 12, 22, 39, 40, 41. R 26, 40. S 148, 172. T 18. W
42, 105.

Royal Engineers:

A 40. B 8, 58, 77. C 9, 65, 75. D 9. E 18, 47, 51. H 61. K 3, 5, 6, 7. L 14,
63, 65, 92. M 16, 17, 30. N 7, 25. S 34, 195. T 15. U 2. W 25, 81, 105, 111. Y
2.

Royal Scots:

C 23. E 24. H 2. N 22. P28. S 96. T 18.

Queen's Royal West Surrey Regt:

B 36, 47. C 24, 79, 95. D 16. E 17. F 6, 8, 22. H 7. P 30. R 34. S 193, 202,
203. W 44, 62, 63, 64, 65, 66, 67, 68, 76, 98.

East Kent Regt:

B 42. C 31. D 4. E 10. H 33. K 4. N 9. R 3. S 15, 122, 141.

King's Own Royal Lancaster Regt:

B 2, 7. L 4.

Northumberland Fusiliers:

A 17, 29. H 4. M 59. N 39. S 23.

Royal Warwickshire Regt:

B 1. H 17. K 15, 17, 18, 19, 20. L 10. N 42, 55. W 26, 27, 28, 29, 30, 59. Y 1.

Royal Fusiliers:

B 90. F 24, 25. H 1. L 73, 86. N 24.

King's Liverpool Regt:

A 23. L 42, 43, 44, 46, 47. M 29. S 143.

Norfolk Regt:

F 4. G 19. N 19, 46, 47, 48. P 7. W 118.

Lincolnshire Regt:

B 78. C 3. D 2. L 29, 30, 33. S 125.

Devonshire Regt:

C 90. D 1, 10, 11. E 49, 50. H 27. K 25, 27. N 14, 15. P 21. T 5, 16.

Suffolk Regt:

E 52. S 187, 188, 189, 190.

Somerset Light Infantry:

C 28, 92. G 20. Q 4. S 114, 115, 127, 128, 129, 132, 133. W 36, 38, 115.

West Yorkshire Regt:

A 25, 36. B 53, 54. C 70. F 1. L 13, 14, 15. P 5. R 22. W 69, 101.

East Yorkshire Regt: B 22. E 19, 20. H 68, 69. P 22. S 84.

Bedfordshire and Hertfordshire Regt:

D 25.

Leicestershire Regt:

L 16. R 36.

Yorkshire Regt:

C 17. E 26. G 26. N 29, 30, 31, 32, 33. S 93, 94. Y 9, 10.

Lancashire Fusiliers:

B 91.

Royal Scots Fusiliers:

A 45. S 98.

Cheshire Regt:

B 27, 55. C 6, 37, 77, 91. E 25. L 34. M 1, 2. N 1, 4, 5. O 14. P 27. S 91.
W 58, 80.

Royal Welsh Fusiliers:

C 22, 93. D 3, 13. E 31. G 24. H 26, 51. L 53. M 49. N 17. R 14, 32, 35, 39.
S 14. W 39, 40.

South Wales Borderers:

C 58.

King's Own Scottish Borderers:

A 32. D 22. M 48. S 48. W 5.

Cameronians (Scottish Rifles):

G 6, 7. H 72. L 2.

Gloucestershire Regt:

B 79. C 13, 34, 35, 76, 96. F 3. G 13. K 29. L 85. M 24, 30, 31. R 18. S 33,
69, 185. W 1, 117.

Worcestershire Regt:

B 87. C 13. D 19, 20. E 48. H 3, 21. K 10, 21. O 2. P 11. R 8. S 179, 182.
W 100, 107, 110, 113, 114.

East Lancashire Regt:

B 95, 96. E 11, 12.

East Surrey Regt:

E 14, 15, 17. H 53. K 28. L 81. R 15, 16, 17, 38. S 202, 203. T 11. W 70, 83, 84.

Duke of Cornwall's Light Infantry:

C 80.

Duke of Wellington's West Riding Regt:

A 22. R 24. S 106. W 60.

Border Regt:

A 43. C 20. H 49. K 1, 31. P 10. Q 1.

Royal Sussex Regt:

B 75, 76. C 64. H 65. M 26, 42. O 7. S 118, 195, 196, 197, 198, 199, 200. T 6. W 20, 49.

Hampshire Regt:

A 14. B 9. C 53. E 9. H 7, 9, 10, 12, 15. K 16. L 93. P 18. R 40. S 111. T 4. V 1. W 62.

South Staffordshire Regt:

B 65. W 7.

Dorset Regt:

S 110. W 72, 85.

South Lancashire Regt:

P 9. R 41. S 149. W 21.

Welsh Regt:

A 2. B 62. L 22. N 2. P 26. S 204.

Black Watch:

F 12. G 23. H 54. M 62.

Oxfordshire and Buckinghamshire Light Infantry:

A 42. B 94. C 87. H 29. L 87. M 3. S 126. W 97, 104.

Essex Regt:

B 4, 6, 56, 57, 89. C 33, 63, 68, 69, 73, 88. E 8, 34, 37, 38, 41, 42, 43, 45. F 9, 17. G 4, 17, 18. H 52. I 2, 3. L 24, 88. M 9, 20, 57. O 3, 6. P 4. S 32, 60, 123, 139. W 8, 10, 43, 47, 48, 79, 102, 116.

Nottinghamshire and Derbyshire Regt:

C 26, 45. D 6, 7, 8. N 52, 53, 54. Q 2. T 10. W 37, 75.

North Lancashire Regt:

A 31. B 39, 41. H 73. N 26.

Northamptonshire Regt:

K 9, 26. M 4. N 21.

Royal Berkshire Regt:

B 20. C 79. D 17. M 8. R 5, 6. W 90, 91, 92, 99.

Royal West Kent Regt:

C 29. S 40, 107. W 46, 52, 53.

King's Own Yorkshire Light Infantry:

D 14. S 104. W 3, 73.

King's Own Shropshire Light Infantry:

B 63. S 119, 120.

Middlesex Regt:

A 10. B 19, 88. C 59. E 2, 3, 29. F 21. H 18, 20. I 15. J 1. K 12. M 10, 33, 34, 35, 36, 37, 38, 39, 40, 41. S 135, 170, 191.

King's Royal Rifle Corps:

K 23. S 12. And all units of the Church Lads Brigade.

Wiltshire Regt:

B 33. W 11, 19, 82.

Manchester Regt:

C 74. H 70. L 17. M 14. S 205.

North Staffordshire Regt:

A 18. B 98. G 25. N 34, 35, 36. R 33. S 163, 164. T 2, 3.

Durham Light Infrantry:

C 46. R 4.

Highland Light Infantry:

A 16. B 17. F 2. G 5, 10.

Gordon Highlanders:

A 7. G 15.

Argyll and Sutherland Highlanders:

A 28. C 12. D 24. H 32. K 30. O 1. R 13. S 169, 176.

Royal Army Service Corps:

A 13. W 23.

Royal Army Medical Corps:

C 1.

Royal East Kent Yeomanry:

A 35.

Sussex Yeomanry:

B 67. S 194.

Warwickshire Yeomanry:

W 32.

Yorkshire Hussars:

Y 11.

Fife and forfar Armoured Car Company:

F 11.

Honourable Artillery Company:

H 62. I 6.

London Regt:

A 19, 34, 37. B 43, 85. C 67, 78, 94. F 23. G 3. K 2, 33. L 8, 19, 21, 61, 62, 70, 71, 72, 73, 74, 77, 78, 80, 83, 86. M 19. N 24, 28. P 6, 23. Q 5, 6. R 1, 25, 31, 37. S 8, 21, 29, 66, 67, 76, 83, 142, 168, 184. T 7. W 14, 45, 63.

Cambridgeshire Regt:

M 22. W 94.

Monmouthshire Regt:

A 1, 8. C 36. E 21. M 52, 53, 54, 56. U 5.

Herefordshire Regt:

H 31.

Hertfordshire Regt:

H 34, 35, 36, 37, 38, 39, 40, 41, 42, 45, 46, 47, 48.

Huntingdonshire Cyclist Battalion:

F 16. K 13.

Inns of Court OTC:

I 9.

Royal Marines:

P 24.

Boys Brigade:

A 3, 4, 5, 6, 11, 15, 21, 24, 44. B 5, 14, 21, 25, 35, 38, 44, 45, 46, 48, 49, 51, 61, 66, 68, 69, 70, 71, 72, 73, 74, 82, 97. C 7, 8, 10, 18, 19, 27, 30, 66, 72, 84. D 5, 12, 15, 26, 27, 23. E 1, 23, 28, 32, 33. F 5, 13, 14. G 1, 2, 8, 16. H 5, 6, 19, 22, 24, 28, 55, 63, 64. I 10, 11. K 32. L 5, 6, 11, 12, 18, 36, 37, 54, 55, 89, 90. M 12, 18, 44, 46, 47, 58. N 8, 16, 20, 50. P 3, 14, 25. R 7, 10, 11, 28, 29, 30. S 9, 16, 37, 38, 55, 58, 65, 68, 85, 112, 116, 137, 140, 144, 145, 146, 147, 165, 171, 173, 174, 177, 178, 183. T 8, 20, 21, 22, 23. W 17, 22, 41, 50, 51, 54, 56, 86, 97.

Church Lads Brigade:

A 12, 20, 38, 39, 41. B 10, 11, 12, 13, 24, 29, 30, 32, 59, 64, 81, 93. C 15, 16, 32, 40, 41, 42, 43, 44, 47, 48, 49, 50, 51, 56, 57, 71. D 29, 30, 31, 32, 33. E 6, 25, 27. G 11, 12. H 30, 56, 57, 58, 59. I 14. L 20, 25, 26, 27, 28, 31, 32, 38, 39, 40, 41, 49, 50, 51, 52, 58, 91. M 11, 21, 27, 41, 51. N 6, 23, 43, 44. O 9, 10, 11, 12, 45. P 2, 8, 15, 16, 17, 29. R 9, 12, 19, 20, 21, 27. S 1, 2, 3, 4, 5, 6, 7, 10, 11, 13, 17, 18, 19, 20, 22, 24, 25, 26, 27, 39, 41, 43, 44, 46, 47, 51, 52, 54, 56, 59, 61, 62, 70, 71, 72, 73, 74, 75, 77, 78, 79, 82, 88, 89, 99, 100, 117, 121, 150, 151, 152, 153, 154, 155, 156, 157, 158, 159, 160, 162, 186. T 1, 9, 12, 13. W 2, 74, 78, 88, 89, 108, 109. Y 4, 5, 6, 7, 8.

Jewish Lads Brigade:

B 31. G 9. L 45, 56, 57. M 13.

APPENDIX B

Army Orders quoted in the Register

1910: 197, 225, 258, 281, 309.

1911: 11, 40, 65, 102, 130, 161, 191, 220, 249, 284, 316, 347.

1912: 11, 41, 75, 109, 143, 177, 207, 233, 260, 290, 320, 343.

1913: 13, 49, 86, 121, 156, 187, 235, 274, 337, 373, 398.

1914: 10, 38, 63, 104, 144, 188, 218, 257, 416, 451, 511.

1915: 41, 79, 109, 139, 225, 261, 302, 343, 381, 430, 457.

1916: 23, 62, 96, 125, 160, 188, 229, 262, 302, 335, 375, 406.

1917: 24, 65, 95, 128, 168, 275, 360.

1918: 51, 111, 149, 173, 209, 240, 307, 342, 373.

1919: 31, 69, 103, 137, 219, 251, 276, 340, 381, 419.

1920: 24, 61, 116, 156, 211, 255, 317, 371, 406, 459, 514, 555.

1921: 25, 72, 118, 184, 226, 271, 323, 365, 398, 452, 493, 527.

1922: 95, 150, 198, 229, 265, 310, 355, 401, 435, 483.

1923: 29.

Front Cover. Church Lads Brigade
                (*Courtesy R.J.Marrion*)

Top left. 1st Cadet Bn. Inns of Court OTC
             (*Courtesy R.J.Marrion*)

Top right. 19th Company, Sheffield Boys
             Brigade

Bellow.   Drums and Bugles, Sussex
             Yeomanry Cadets

www.ingramcontent.com/pod-product-compliance
Lightning Source LLC
Chambersburg PA
CBHW081552110426
42743CB00048BA/3137